Understanding
French Verse

Understanding

French Verse

A GUIDE FOR SINGERS

David Hunter

OXFORD
UNIVERSITY PRESS
2005

OXFORD
UNIVERSITY PRESS

Oxford University Press, Inc., publishes works that further
Oxford University's objective of excellence
in research, scholarship, and education.

Oxford   New York
Auckland   Cape Town   Dar es Salaam   Hong Kong   Karachi
Kuala Lumpur   Madrid   Melbourne   Mexico City   Nairobi
New Delhi   Shanghai   Taipei   Toronto

With offices in
Argentina   Austria   Brazil   Chile   Czech Republic   France   Greece
Guatemala   Hungary   Italy   Japan   Poland   Portugal   Singapore
South Korea   Switzerland   Thailand   Turkey   Ukraine   Vietnam

Published by Oxford University Press, Inc.
198 Madison Avenue, New York, New York, 10016

www.oup.com

Oxford is a registered trademark of Oxford University Press

Library of Congress Cataloging-in-Publication Data
Hunter, David, 1955–
Understanding French verse : a guide for singers / David Hunter.
    p. cm.
Includes bibliographical references and index.
ISBN-13 978-0-19-517716-9
ISBN 0-19-517716-9
1. French language—Versification.   2. Singing—Diction.   I. Title.
PC2511 .H86 2005
841.009—dc22   2004063558

9 8 7 6 5 4 3 2

Printed in the United States of America
on acid-free paper

To Derek Hammond-Stroud and Clive Scott

Acknowledgments

This is a short guide, but many people have contributed to its publication. Derek Hammond-Stroud and Clive Scott have been inspiring teachers. Without their example, the writing would almost certainly not have been started. Richard Stokes has been extremely generous with his help. I would like to thank him, in particular, for granting me permission to use his translations. A number of friends have provided encouragement and comments. I would mention especially Colin Bailey, Nick Edwards, Richard Mason, Florence Pougnet, and Xu Yee-Ruh. Nick Wetton was an invaluable source of help in preparing the manuscript, and my contacts at Oxford University Press, Kim Robinson, Eve Bachrach, and Linda Donnelly, have been unfailingly responsive. Finally, I owe a great debt to my wife, Oonagh Gay, who, despite her own writing commitments, has been wonderfully supportive at all stages in the preparation of the guide.

I would like to acknowledge the use of the following extracts in the guide:

Henri de Régnier, from "Chanson," in *La sandale ailée* (Mercure de France, 1906), © Mercure de France. Reprinted by permission of the publisher.

Robert Desnos, "Dans la nuit il y a naturellement les sept merveilles du monde . . ." from *Corps et biens* (1930), © Éditions Gallimard, Paris, 1930. Reprinted by permission of the publisher.

Paul Éluard, from "Rayons des yeux et des soleils," in *Œuvres complètes, 1* (1968), © Éditions Gallimard, Paris, 1968. Reprinted by permission of the publisher; 'Jacques Villon' from *Œuvres complètes, 2* (1968), © Éditions Gallimard, Paris, 1968.

Acknowledgments

Rosemonde Gérard, from "Villanelle des petits canards," in *Les Pipeaux* (Librairie A. Lemerre, 1889). Reprinted by permission of Éditions Bernard Grasset.

Paul Verlaine, from "Art poetique," in *Selected Poems*, translated by Joanna Richardson (Penguin Books, 1974). Reprinted by permission of Curtis Brown Ltd. on behalf of the translator.

Every effort has been made to locate the holders of rights to poems that appear in this book; we regret if any have been overlooked.

Contents

1. Why This Guide?   3

2. The Basics of the French Line   6

3. Common French Meters   17

4. Stanzas   26

5. Sonnets, rondels, and other fixed forms   41

6. Rhyme   55

7. Free verse   69

Appendix 1. Commentaries on four poems   81

     Adieux de l'hôtesse arabe   81

     Le colibri   85

     En sourdine   89

     Montparnasse   92

Appendix 2. Poems and songs discussed in the guide   96

Appendix 3. A brief history of French versification   101

Glossary of technical terms   103

Notes   108

Suggestions for further reading   115

Index   117

Understanding
French Verse

1 ✒ Why This Guide?

*I*N *MASTER CLASSES* and in textbooks on song, young singers are frequently reminded to take great care over the poetic texts of the songs they wish to perform. "Study the poem away from the music, so that you know what the words really mean," advised the great French singer Claire Croiza.[1] "The literary text deserves the same care, the same scrupulous accuracy, in short the same respect that is demanded by the musical text," wrote her equally distinguished compatriot, Pierre Bernac.[2]

Such advice—apparently uncontentious—begs a fundamental question. Does one study or read a French poem in the same way as one would study or read a poem in another language? Many English speakers who have struggled with the apparent mysteries of French verse would doubtless answer with a resounding "No."

THE FOCUS FOR THE GUIDE

This guide provides an introduction to the basics of French versification. It is aimed at singers, composers, and other musicians who want to understand more about the French texts with which they are working.

The various chapters of the guide address questions such as, How does a line of French verse work? What are the characteristics of the main meters? What's special about rhyme in French? How does a French sonnet differ from its English counterpart? The examples used to answer these questions are all taken from well-known mélodies.

Is any of this important? Does it matter that Verlaine's "En sourdine," set to music by Debussy among others, uses a 7-syllable meter rather than the more common 8-syllable or "octosyllable" and that all the rhymes are "masculine"? Does it help to know that in Sully Prudhomme's poem "Le long du quai," set by Fauré as "Les berceaux," the rhyme scheme changes in the third stanza? There are good reasons for believing it may.

First, poets such as Verlaine and Sully Prudhomme clearly took great pains over their versification and would have expected contemporary readers to notice the results. "En sourdine," for instance, is an exquisitely crafted poem that sends out strong messages through its formal structure (which I explore later in this guide) about how it might be interpreted. An understanding of versification should allow us to approach the poetry of the mélodie more creatively.

Second, among contemporary readers were the composers of the mélodie themselves, in general a highly literate group. Fauré, we know, won prizes for literary studies on two occasions during his years at the Niedermeyer school and was able to turn his hand to elegant light verse.[3] Debussy, Chausson, Chabrier, and later Poulenc were all the friends and associates of leading contemporary poets. At the very least, one would expect such composers to have had a strong sense of how French poetry worked at a formal level and possibly even to have reflected some of this understanding in their musical settings.

THE SCOPE OF THE GUIDE

A guide of this type cannot cover everything. I have deliberately concentrated on the formal "mechanics" of versification and not considered aspects of poetry such as use of metaphor or poetic voice. The guide also deals primarily with regular verse, although I have touched on free verse in the final chapter. The complexities of prose and the prose poem I have left for another day.

There also continue to be lively academic arguments over almost every topic covered by the guide, including the very nature of French verse. I have tried, where possible, to reflect these debates in my text, but inevitably I have had to simplify what is a complex subject. For readers who want to explore further, I have provided detailed notes and appended Suggestions for Further Reading.

Finally, the guide decidedly does not profess to offer any special insights into the magical process by which a poem becomes a mélodie. However sensitive to poetry, composers are pragmatic beings who select, manipulate, and sometimes even destroy formal poetic structures when they feel it is appropriate. (Fauré is a notable example.) Most students of French verse can only stand back and admit how little they understand about the transformation of poem into song.

Within these limitations, I hope you find the guide informative, useful, and stimulating. If it provokes some new ideas or insights, it will have served its purpose.

2 ❧ The Basics of the French Line

How SHOULD WE APPROACH a line of regular French verse?

A good starting point for an exploration is that most famous of French meters, the alexandrine, which from the seventeenth century until the end of the nineteenth was widely used in every genre of verse.[1] More than one third of the poems in the first five collections published by Verlaine (the French poet most frequently set to music) are in alexandrines, albeit not always regular ones.

What, then, are its main features and what does it tell us about French verse in general?

THE STRUCTURE OF THE ALEXANDRINE

The rules governing the alexandrine in its traditional form are simply stated:

- The line has 12 syllables, divided into two equal 6-syllable sections or "hemistiches" around a central juncture or "caesura." The caesura is usually marked in scansion by two oblique lines //.
- There are fixed, obligatory stresses—usually called "accents"—on the sixth and twelfth syllables, that is at the caesura and at the end of the line. There are usually two additional secondary stresses in the line, one in each hemistich.
- These secondary stresses can fall on any syllable not already accented. Their location is indicated in scansion by a single oblique line or "coupe" that comes immediately after the stressed syllable.[2]

A couple of examples will illustrate these points.

> Les jasmins / de Mossoul // les fleurs / de l'oranger
> 1 2 3   4 5 6   7 8   9 10 11 12

> The jasmines of Mosul, the orange blossom

In this line from Leconte de Lisle's "Les roses d'Ispahan," set by Fauré, the fixed stresses are on Mos**soul** and oran**ger**. The secondary stresses fall on the third and eighth syllables, jas**mins** and **fleurs**, giving the line a subdivision of syllables that might be described as $3 + 3 + 2 + 4$.

Compare the second line of Baudelaire's poem "Recueillement," set by Debussy:

> Tu réclamais / le Soir; // il descend; / le voici
> 1 2 3 4 5   6   7 8 9   10 11 12

> You longed for Evening; it is falling; now

In this line, the main stresses fall, as expected, on **Soir** and voi**ci** and the secondary stresses on récla**mais** and des**cend**. The pattern here might be notated as $4 + 2 + 3 + 3$.

This traditional type of alexandrine is commonly referred to as the "alexandrin tétramètre" because its structure typically incorporates four rhythmic segments or "measures." Overall, it offers the poet a total of twenty-five different combinations[3]—a tremendous variety in what can appear, at first sight, a rather forbidding and rigid form.

SOME DIFFERENCES BETWEEN FRENCH AND ENGLISH VERSE

My brief analysis of these two alexandrines has hinted at a fundamental difference between French and English.

French words do not have the innate stress of their counterparts in English, in which words of more than one syllable typically have a defined point of emphasis—water, propel, magnanimous, tolerate—and one-syllable words that are grammatically significant (nouns, verbs, adjectives, adverbs) are also likely to attract stress.

Instead, a French word's position in a phrase will normally determine whether or not it bears an accent. The general rule is that stress falls on the last accentuable syllable in any word group—un joli ma**tin**, but un matin bru**meux**. French stress is therefore phrase-related, whereas stress in English remains linked primarily to individual words.[4]

This distinction has important consequences for the two verse traditions.

FRENCH AND ENGLISH VERSE APPROACH METER AND RHYTHM
IN DIFFERENT WAYS

Most verse in English has been built upon regular patterns of stressed and unstressed syllables. These patterns have traditionally been scanned as "feet," sequences of which combine to form a meter.

Hence the classic iambic pentameter (5 foot meter) with its familiar ti-tum beat:

> And darkly bright are bright in dark direct(ed)[5]
> x / x / x / x / x /

Or the popular iambic tetrameter (4 foot meter):

> And there for me the apple tree[6]
> x / x / x / x /

(where x represents an unstressed syllable and / a stressed syllable).

As these examples suggest, feet act as repeated metrical units within an English poem around which individual words, with their particular stress patterns, are arranged. Endless repetition of exactly the same accentual sequence would, of course, be monotonous; poets will typically create rhythmic variations within their chosen meters by inserting other types of metrical unit (for instance, substituting a trochaic for an iambic foot in a particular line), omitting syllables, or using similar devices. Nevertheless, one still senses an underlying metrical pulse or beat.

French verse, on the other hand, contains no such repeated units.[7] As we have already seen, a few important points in the line, such as the sixth and twelfth syllables in the regular alexandrine, act as metrical anchors and attract stress as of right. Otherwise poets are free to create anew the accentual pattern of each line, primarily through the way in which they manipulate the syntax of the text, since secondary stress points will usually coincide with the ends of word groups.

In very crude terms, therefore, in regular English verse, words are broadly fitted to a pre-existing meter, albeit with conventional rhythmic variations, whereas in French verse, with its relative paucity of metrical features, the rhythmic shape of each line is influenced to a much greater degree by the way in which the poet chooses to dispose the words, and the pattern of one line does not predict the pattern of the next. Readers from an English-speaking tradition must be careful, as a consequence, not to discover in French texts a regular "beat" that is not there.[8]

IN REGULAR FRENCH VERSE, SYLLABLE COUNT IS CRUCIAL

Although, in principle, an English iambic pentameter has 10 syllables and a tetrameter 8, in practice the syllable count in individual lines can vary without the ear being unduly troubled. For instance, in Tennyson's "The Kraken," set by Britten, the iambic pentameter is undisturbed by lines such as

Battening upon huge seaworms in his sleep

which strictly contains 11 syllables.[9] The basic meter still carries the poem along.

French verse, on the other hand, with its lack of a regular rhythmic pulse, has traditionally relied on a precise syllable count (as well as features such as end rhyme, which I discuss in Chapter 6) both to highlight its status as poetry and also to distinguish different meters.

Differences in line length matter tremendously in French. The 12-syllable alexandrine and the 10-syllable decasyllable are fundamentally different lines, each with its own history, structure, and traditions. Even greater divergences have been perceived between lines with an even number of syllables ("pairs") and those with an odd number of syllables ("impairs").

I examine the more common meters in more detail in the next chapter. For the moment, I want to address a question that is clearly a crucial issue in a syllable-based versification, "What counts as a syllable and when?"

COUNTING SYLLABLES: THE "MUTE E"

The most important debates revolve around the treatment of the syllables "e," "ent," or "es," which end many French words. Théophile Gautier's short line "Ma belle amie est morte," from his poem "Lamento" (set by both Berlioz and Fauré), contains three such syllables.

These syllables are known by the terms "e atone" or "e muet" ("mute e"). They have been trumpeted as one of the greatest expressive resources of French verse, lending the line a mellifluousness and flexibility it would otherwise lack.[10]

The basic rules for handling the mute e in verse are as follows:

- An "e," "ent," or "es" at the end of a line is *not* included in the tally of syllables, even though in poetry (as opposed to normal speech) it might attract some pronunciation.[11] So the word "morte" in Gautier's line above only counts as one syllable. Words such as "immense" or "descendre" at the end of a line would count as two syllables. In scansion, the uncounted syllables are sometimes put in brackets, thus: "mort(e)."

- On the other hand, a mute e *within* the line does count and in recitation would almost certainly attract some pronunciation. In Gautier's line "Comme dans la nature," the "e" at the end of "comme" would therefore be included in the tally of syllables (the "e" in "nature," of course, would not, as it terminates the line).

- The main exception to the rule on the mute e *within* the line arises when a word ending with an "e" is immediately followed by another word that starts with a vowel or unaspirated "h."[12] In these circumstances, the mute e is suppressed or "elided.'" So in Gautier's line "Ah! comm(e) ell(e) était bell(e)" none of the syllables in brackets would be included in the syllable count. Note that this does *not* apply to the endings "ent" or "es" within the line, since they finish in consonants and therefore cannot be elided.

So by now it should have become apparent that the Gautier poem from which all the lines in this section are taken is in a 6-syllable ("hexasyllabic") meter.

> Ma bell(e) ami(e) est mort(e)
> 1 2 3 4 5 6

My dearest love is dead

> Comme dans la natur(e)
> 1 2 3 4 5 6

How everything in nature

> Ah! comm(e) ell(e) était bell(e)
> 1 2 3 4 5 6

Ah! how beautiful she was

There are other rules governing syllable count, particularly concerning how to treat the contiguous vowels in words such as "pied" or "suave": should they count as one syllable or two?[13] These rules are often highly complex, drawing on the historic roots of specific words and the prevailing poetic practice at various points in the history of French verse, and are beyond the scope of this guide.

For practical purposes, if the reader is unsure about the treatment of a particular word, the best approach is to count the syllables in other lines of the poem and work backwards. We can assume, for instance, that there are 7 syllables in this line from Verlaine's poem "En sourdine" (and 4 in the word "persuader") because the rest of the poem is in a 7-syllable meter:

> Laissons nous persuader
> 1   2   3   4 56 7

> Let us both succumb

SCANNING THE MUTE E

The mute e raises important issues about how we read and scan French lines. We said earlier that stresses in French verse generally fall on the last *accentuable* syllable of a word group. The mute e, despite the fact that it often counted as a syllable within the line, is not considered adequate to bear an accent.[14] So how do we approach a line in which one or more word groups end with a mute e?

The answer is that any division within the line is generally held to fall before the mute e, and the syllable itself is counted as part of the following word group, even if this appears to divide an individual word in two. So the following line from Lamartine's poem "Le vallon," set by Gounod, would be scanned thus:

> Un asi/le d'un jour // pour attend/re la mort
> 1   2 3 4   5   6   7   8 9   10 11 12

> One day's refuge to wait for death

The overall pattern is 3 + 3 + 3 + 3, the "coupes enjambantes" on "asile" and "attendre" (as these sorts of divisions are technically known) contributing in this example to an evenness and uneventfulness that suitably reflects the poet's exhausted emotional state.

There is one major exception to this practice. In a very few cases, a word ending in a mute e is deemed to be separate enough from the word(s) that follow, as a result of punctuation, syntax, or meaning, to justify what is known technically as a "coupe lyrique." In these circumstances, the mute e is counted as part of the preceding word group for the purposes of scansion. Invocations are a prime source for this sort of coupe, which typically creates a pause in the flow of the verse. Jean de La Ville de Mirmont's poem "Diane, Séléné," set by Fauré, provides a good example.

Diane, / Séléné, // lu/ne de beau métal
1 2 3   4 5 6   7 8 9 10 11 12

Diane, Selene, moon of beautiful metal

The scansion here gives a 3' + 3 reading of the first hemistich,[15] emphasizing the pause of wonderment after the magical name of Diana is pronounced and underlining the apposition (and syllabic equality) of Diane and Séléné. A "coupe enjambante" seems more appropriate to the second half of the line to emphasize the smooth, uninterrupted and metallic surface of the moon.

SOME FINAL THOUGHTS ON THE FRENCH LINE

We need to touch on three other issues to complete our brief survey of the French line.

TREATMENT OF THE MUTE E AFTER THE CAESURA

We have seen that a mute e cannot bear an accent in regular verse and therefore cannot, for instance, be positioned on the sixth syllable of an alexandrine.

By the nineteenth century it was also considered bad practice for the second hemistich of a line to begin with such a syllable. If poets wished to place a word such as "morte" at the caesura, they had to ensure that the mute e in the word was capable of being elided and did not, therefore, trail over in the latter part of the line.

Lamartine's poem "Le vallon," mentioned earlier, offers three examples of this practice:

D'ici je vois la vi(e)[16] // à travers un nuag(e)
1 2 3 4   5 6   7 8 9   10 11 12

From here I can see life, across a cloud

Repose-toi, mon âm(e) // en ce dernier asil(e)
1 2 3 4   5   6   7 8 9 10 11 12

Rest, my soul, in this final refuge

Déclinent comme l'ombr(e) // au penchant
1 2 3   4   5 6   7   8   9
   des coteaux
   10 11 12

Draw in like darkness on the hills

As can be seen, the first word in each of the second hemistiches starts with a vowel, allowing the mute e at the end of the previous word to be elided.[17]

ENJAMBMENT

Enjambment—the running of the sense and syntax of one line into the next —is a feature of both French and English verse. However, whereas in English it is a relatively unexceptional device, since the verse is carried along from line to line by the underlying meter, in French, with its more autonomous lines, enjambment carries a greater shock value.

For example, in Verlaine's poem "Clair de lune" (set by many composers), the contrast between the joyous activities of music-making and dancing and the revelers' melancholy is abruptly brought to our attention by the enjambment "quasi"/ "tristes":

> Jouant du luth, et dansant, et quasi
> Tristes, sous leur déguisements fantasques

> Playing the lute and dancing and almost
> Sad beneath their fanciful disguises

Enjambments can span lines (and potentially stanzas—see Chapter 7) but may also be found within lines. In Jean de La Ville de Mirmont's poem "Vaisseaux . . .," for instance, an enjambment straddles the caesura of the first alexandrine:

> Vaisseaux, nous vous aurons // aimés en pure perte

> Ships, we shall have loved you to no avail

As is clear from both the examples above, the act of enjambment typically isolates a particular word or phrase ("tristes" in the Verlaine and "aimés" in the Mirmont), encouraging the reader to give it both greater attention and extra stress. The isolated word or phrase after the enjambment is known technically as the "rejet."[18]

POETIC LANGUAGE

The placing of two vowels side by side, creating hiatus, is generally accepted within words but frowned upon as "unpoetic" between words. This means that many common combinations of French words are rarely found in traditional verse, including "tu as," "j'ai eu," "peu à peu" and so on. The word "et" (*and*) counts as a vowel for these purposes, despite the fact it ends in a consonant, and many potential usages are banned, such as "et arbres."[19]

The rules of good verse may discourage certain combinations of words, but poetic practice also allows certain constructions that would seem at best labored in normal speech. The elaborate inversion of word order in the fourth line of Verlaine's poem "Green," set by Debussy, Fauré, and Hahn, is a good example:

Et qu'à vos yeux si beaux l'humble présent soit doux

And may the humble gift please your lovely eyes

Readers will also come across "poetic" spellings of common words — "encor" rather than "encore" or "avecque" instead of "avec" — which can be particularly useful for keeping to the rules of syllable counting. Overall, we would expect poetry to be read or spoken more slowly, with more care for rhythm and junctures and more emphasis on the mute e.

3 ✒️ Common French Meters

WE HAVE SEEN THAT syllable count matters in French verse—indeed, it is the feature that distinguishes different meters.

In the first part of this chapter, I look at common meters in more detail. In each case, I summarize the meter's history and structure, as well as the interpretative issues it raises. The second part of the chapter examines mixed meters and the "vers impair" (meters with odd numbers of syllables).

An initial distinction often made in commentary on French verse is between "vers composés" (lines of 9 syllables or more) and "vers simples" (lines of 8 syllables or less). As will become apparent, "vers composés" generally have a more complicated internal structure, involving a caesura.

THE ALEXANDRINE

We have already encountered the alexandrine or 12-syllable line in Chapter 2. Its influence on French poetry cannot be underestimated. Throughout most of the nineteenth century and, indeed, into the twentieth, the alexandrine remained the template against which verse was measured. The most frequent meter in Apollinaire's collection *Alcools*, published in 1913, remains the alexandrine, although individual lines may break traditional rules in some way.[1]

Such is the impact of the alexandrine that some critics have argued that the meter promotes a particular way of apprehending the world in the poems where it is deployed, the central caesura encouraging the perception of relationships of symmetry, parallelism, or antithesis between the two halves of each line.[2] Certainly, the structure of an alexandrine such as Jean de La Ville de Mirmont's

La mer est infini(e) // et mes rêves sont fous

The sea is boundless and my dreams are wild

(set by Fauré) seems to suggest a causal link, an identity even, between the vastness of the sea and the free-ranging nature of the poet's dreams.

Other commentators have discerned a distinct curve or convexity in the shape of the line—the alexandrine as an arch with the caesura forming the keystone.[3] In this analysis, the first hemistich of an alexandrine would typically be characterized by a rising intonation and a forward momentum, whereas the second hemistich would display falling intonation and more inward-looking or restrained movement.

Although these ideas may seem rather esoteric, they raise interesting questions of interpretation. Take the following line, for instance, from Grandmougin's poem "Rencontre," set by Fauré:

J'étais triste et pensif // quand je t'ai rencontré(e)

I was sad and pensive when I met you

Does the fact that the meeting between the poet and his beloved falls into the second half of the alexandrine already hint that the outcome will not be a happy one? Does the placing of "triste et pensif" in the first hemistich suggest that the poet is rather wallowing in his unhappiness, perhaps as a fruitful creative state?[4]

THE DECASYLLABLE

The first appearance of the 10-syllable or decasyllabic line has been dated to as far back as the eleventh century. Its use in the *Chanson de*

Roland established the decasyllable firmly in epic poetry and it became the preferred line for lyric verse during the medieval period.

By the seventeenth century, the decasyllable had been dethroned by the alexandrine and, until well into the following century, it was relegated primarily to lighter verse. However, by the end of the eighteenth century it had reappeared in lyric poetry and it is found often in the works of nineteenth-century poets such as Gautier and Leconte de Lisle and, later, Verlaine.

The decasyllable exists in a number of different forms. The classic division of its 10 syllables is 4 + 6, with a caesura after the fourth syllable. In this form, three accents per line is the norm. Clément Marot's "Chanson XIII," set by Enescu as "Languir me fais," provides a good example:

> Mais je me **plains** // de l'en**nuy** que j'ac**quiers**
> 1 2 3 4 5 6 7 8 9 10

> But I complain of the grief I suffer

Victor Hugo's poem "Oh! quand je dors," set by Liszt, has a similar structure:

> Pos(e) un bai**ser**, // et **d'ang**e deviens **femm**(e)
> 1 2 3 4 5 6 7 8 9 10

> Place a kiss and be transformed from angel into
> woman

This structure gives the line a distinctive shape, in which a rapid, first section is followed by a more measured and reflective second section.

A 6 + 4 form of the decasyllable is also found, but usually only as an accompanying meter, in texts where the 4 + 6 form is present too.[5] Much more important for our purposes is the 5 + 5 structure with a central caesura. Leconte de Lisle's "Le colibri," set by Chausson, offers an example,

Le vert colibri // le roi des collin(es)
1 2   3 4 5   6 7 8 9 10

The green humming-bird, the king of the hills

as does his poem "La rose," set by Fauré,

Je dirai la ros(e) // au plis gracieux
1 2 3 4   5   6   7   8 9 10

I shall speak of the rose with its graceful petals

The 5 + 5 form of the decasyllable was employed in medieval times for song texts and popular poems and reappeared in the formal lyric poetry of the nineteenth century. It creates an even balance of syllables within the line, but it may also contribute to rhythmic destabilization and uncertainty, since it is not always obvious whether to give a particular line three accents, as is normal in other forms of the decasyllable, or four accents, in order to reflect the syllabic equality of the two hemistiches.

In the first line of "Le colibri," for example, it seems clear that both "**roi**" and "col**line**'" would be stressed, as would "coli**bri**." But what of "vert"? Do we run over the word quickly, seeing it as a not very significant attribute of the bird? Or do we place a stress on the word, particularly as it is placed before the noun, making it something much more important—a symbol of youth and freshness that makes the bird's eventual, poetic death that much more affecting?

THE OCTOSYLLABLE

The French 8-syllable or octosyllabic line has a long and complex history, dating back as far as the tenth century according to some scholars. During the sixteenth and seventeenth centuries, it was mainly associated with minor genres, but by the end of the eighteenth century it had regained its place in lyric poetry. It is generally considered to have been the most commonly employed meter, after the alexandrine, during the nineteenth century and later came to be associated with twentieth century poets such as Apollinaire.

The octosyllable has only one fixed accent, on the eighth syllable. As the longest vers simple, it has no obligatory caesura, unlike the alexandrine and decasyllable. Lahor's poem "Chanson triste," set by Duparc, is an example:

> Dans ton cœur dort un clair de **lun**(e)
> 1   2   3   4   5   6 7 8

> Moonlight slumbers in your heart

The octosyllable lies between the three-accent pattern typical of the classic decasyllable and the two-accent pattern of the 6-syllable or "hexasyllabic" line. Indeed, some commentators have suggested that there is a fundamental ambiguity about the octosyllable, which allows each reader much more scope to devise or discern different stress patterns within this meter than would be the case in more formally structured lines such as the alexandrine.[6]

In Lahor's octosyllable above, for instance, we could stress just the words "cœur" and "lune," infusing the line with a lunar calm. Alternatively, we could choose to add an accent on the word "dort" (making three stresses in total) in order to emphasize the unusual image and to prefigure the main theme of the poem—the beloved as an oasis of peace for the world-weary poet.

Such flexibility perhaps explains why the octosyllable has a reputation for being mercurial and mobile, and why it is the meter that is commonly thought to be closest to the normal speech patterns of French. It may also underpin the strong connections that the line has traditionally had with song.

SHORTER LINES

Many shorter lines are also found in the poetry of the mélodie. We have already seen Gautier using the hexasyllable or 6-syllable line, whose popularity may have something to do with its resemblance to half an alexandrine. Verlaine's poem "Il pleure dans mon cœur," set by Debussy, offers another instance of this meter.

Examples of the use of even shorter lines include Verlaine's 4-syllable poem "La lune blanche," set by both Fauré and Hahn, and Saint-Saëns's song "Le pas d'armes du roi Jean," based on the poem of the same name by Victor Hugo, which is perhaps the best-known setting of a 3-syllable line:

> Par saint-Gill(es)
> 1   2   3
> Viens-nous-en
> 1   2   3

> By Saint Giles,
> Let us set out

In one way, however, these examples are unusual, since shorter lines are generally used to complement longer lines rather than as meters in their own right. In such circumstances, the shorter line—particularly those of 4 syllables or less—will often serve as a refrain or echo, as in Duparc's setting of Sully Prudhomme's poem "Soupir":

> Mais, fidèle, toujours l'attendre,
> Toujours l'aimer.

> But faithful, always to wait for her,
> Always to love her.

In other poems, such as Hugo's "Le papillon et la fleur," set by Fauré, the shorter meter offers a commentary or even a light-hearted burlesque on its longer partner:

Mais, hélas, l'air t'emporte et la terre m'enchaîne,
   Sort cruel!

But alas! The breeze bears you away, the earth holds
   me fast.
Cruel fate!

In the early part of the nineteenth century, when different meters were deployed within the same poem, typically no more than two would be used. However, later in the century, poets began to introduce greater variety into their verse. Banville's "La dernière pensée de Weber," which mixes 3-, 7-, and 8-syllable lines and was set by Debussy as "Nuit d'étoiles," is a good example of this trend.

Finally, it is unusual for two of the longer meters or vers composés to be combined—alexandrines with decasyllables for example. It is much more common to find a vers composé mixed with a vers simple. Examples include the following:

- Hugo's "Adieux de l'hôtesse arabe," set by Bizet: 12- and 8-syllable lines
- Gounod's "L'absent" to words by the composer: 12- and 6-syllable lines
- Leconte de Lisle's "Nanny," set by Chausson: 10- and 8-syllable lines
- Sully Prudhomme's "Au bord de l'eau," set by Fauré: 10- and 4-syllable lines

Alternatively, vers simples may be combined with other vers simples, as in the following examples:

- Gautier's "Lamento," set by Duparc: 8- and 4-syllable lines
- Verlaine's "À Clymène," set by Fauré: 6- and 4-syllable lines
- Richepin's "Au cimetière," also set by Fauré: 6- and 2-syllable lines

THE VERS IMPAIR

Something should be said about meters with odd-numbered syllables—vers impairs. Lines of 3, 5, 7, 9, 11, or 13 syllables do feature in the history of French verse—Ronsard's 7-syllable poem "À Cassandre" (set by Leguerney as "À sa maîtresse") is one instance—but they are relatively scarce and do not have the same weight of established tradition behind them as their even-numbered counterparts.

Where such meters are used, they are often associated with music. The 5-syllable line, for instance, is the meter of many popular songs ("Au clair de la lune," to give one example) and is found during the eighteenth century in light verses going under the heading of "Chanson." During the nineteenth century, poet-songwriters, such as Béranger, often used this meter in their work. Other vers impairs have similar historic links to song.

When we find Hugo using a 7-syllable meter in "Mes vers fuiraient, doux et frêles" (set by Hahn), or Baudelaire combining 5- and 7-syllable lines in "L'Invitation au voyage" (set by both Duparc and Chabrier), we can almost imagine the poems as serenades well before they were set to music.

Later in the nineteenth century, the vers impair took on another layer of meaning. Verlaine, in particular, while often continuing to use these meters in poems with musical themes,[7] promoted the use of the impair as part of a deliberate attempt to create a fluid, unstable and anti-rhetorical form of poetry, in contrast to the more familiar even-numbered meters traditionally favored by French poets.

The most famous statement of his credo comes in his poem "Art poétique," itself written in 9-syllable lines:

> De la musique avant toute chose,
> Et pour cela préfère l'Impair
> Plus vague et plus soluble dans l'air,
> Sans rien en lui qui pèse ou qui pose.

> Above all things be musical,
> And so prefer uneven lines
> Where nothing settles or confines,
> Dissolving, insubstantial.[8]

When we come across the vers impair in the songs of Fauré, Debussy, Hahn, and other composers, we should be aware of its significance to modern verse practice in late nineteenth century French poetry.

4 ✤ Stanzas

IN FRENCH VERSE, just as in English, poets commonly group their individual lines to form larger patterns. These patterns may appear as subdivisions of the poem—as stanzas, or "strophes" as they are usually called in French; or the poem as a whole may follow a traditional pattern, or variation of it, such as sonnet form.

Poets create such patterns for many reasons: to give the reader points of reference within the structure of the poem; to offer moments of drama, pause, or reflection within the flow of the verse; to set up force-fields of similarity and contrast that generate meaning. In regular French verse, where rhyme is an important method of linking different lines, stanzaic and other patterns are intimately bound up with the acoustic structure of the poem. And, as stanzas have traditionally had a unity of both theme and structure, they necessarily have a relationship with patterns of meaning and syntax.

In this chapter, I describe some of the more common stanzaic patterns in French verse, using examples drawn from the mélodie. Chapter 5 then looks at various "fixed forms" such as the sonnet and rondel.[1] In both cases, I have tried to highlight how these ways of structuring a poem may contribute to its meaning, accepting that the precise interpretations we generate will vary from poem to poem. The intricacies of rhyme itself are explored in more detail in Chapter 6.

THE COUPLET

The couplet, known as "rimes plates" in French, is a pair of rhyming lines. Jean Dominique's "Le don silencieux," set by Fauré, offers an example.

Je mettrai mes doux mains sur ma bouche, pour
    taire   *a*
Ce que je voudrais tant vous dire, âme bien chère! *a*

I shall place my two hands over my mouth, to
    silence
What I so wish to tell you, dearest soul!

The French couplet dates back many hundreds of years. It reached its zenith between the seventeenth and nineteenth centuries, a period during which it was used widely in verse tragedies as well as in all manner of lyric and satirical verse.

In traditional usage, pairs of lines followed one another without a break, creating a pattern *aabbccddeeff* and so on, as in Gounod's setting of Jean-Antoine de Baïf's "O ma belle rebelle."

O ma belle rebelle,   *a*
Las! que tu m'es cruelle!   *a*
Ou quand d'un doux souris,   *b*
Larron de mes espris,   *b*
Ou quand d'une parolle   *c*
Mignardetement molle   *c*

  . . . .

O my rebellious belle,
Alas, how cruel you are,
When with a sweet smile
You steal my soul,
Or with a soft
Seductive word,

  . . . .

However, during the nineteenth century, poets such as Baudelaire and Verlaine began to insert blank lines between the pairs of rhyming lines, forming isolated couplets (technically known as "distiques") that can be notated *aa bb cc dd ee* etc. Fauré's setting of Van Lerberghe's "Quand tu plonges tes yeux dans mes yeux" follows this practice:

Si tu frôles mes cheveux,	*a*
Je n'existe plus qu'en eux.	*a*
Si ta main effleure mes seins,	*b*
J'y monte comme un feu soudain.[2]	*b*

When you stroke my hair,
I no longer exist but there.

If your hand but brushes my breasts,
I quicken there like a sudden fire.

The most notable feature of the couplet is the rapid return of the rhyme, the first line immediately answered by the second. In certain circumstances, this can convey a sense of self-confidence and assurance—the world in its rightful order. The narrator in Verlaine's "La dure épreuve va finir," set by Hahn as "La bonne chanson," aspires to just such a state.

J'ai tu les paroles amères	*a*
Et banni les sombres chimères.	*a*

I have silenced bitter words
And banished dark imaginings.

However, the couplet may also contribute to a sense of pressure and enclosure, suggesting an inability to escape a tightly drawn noose. In one of the most famous of all mélodies, Debussy's setting of Verlaine's "Colloque sentimental," the couplet form, combined with the poet's skillful use of blank space and punctuation, serves to isolate the lines of verse and surround them with silence, vividly illustrating the despairing and lacerating embrace in which the protagonists are locked.

> – Qu'il était bleu, le ciel, et grand, l'espoir!   *a*
> – L'espoir a fui, vaincu, vers le ciel noir.   *a*

> – How blue the sky, how hopes ran high!
> – Hope has fled, vanquished, to the black sky.

THE QUATRAIN

The quatrain or 4-line stanza is one of the most frequently used forms in the verse of the mélodie.

An *abab* rhyme scheme, known technically as "rimes croisées," is most common, with a tendency to place the strongest punctuation at the end of the second and fourth lines. Hugo's poem "Quand la nuit n'est pas étoilée," set by Hahn, is an example.

> L'ombre et l'abîme ont un mystère   *a*
> Que nul mortel ne pénétra;   *b*
> C'est Dieu qui leur dit de se taire   *a*
> Jusqu'au jour où tout parlera!   *b*

> The dark and the abyss hold mysteries
> Unfathomed by human kind;
> It is God who bids them be silent
> Until the day when all shall speak!

For some commentators, stanzas such as this offer a sequence of cinematographic "shots" that give the verse a forward momentum and narrative dynamic, although sometimes with hesitations.[3] The scheme is even-paced, without the conflict that may characterize other patterns.

The other main pattern for the quatrain is *abba*, referred to in French as "rimes embrassées." Tristan l'Hermite uses this type of quatrain in his poem "Le promenoir des deux amants," set by Debussy.

Auprès de cette grotte sombre   *a*
Où l'on respire un air si doux,   *b*
L'onde lutte avec les cailloux,   *b*
Et la lumière avecque l'ombre.[4]   *a*

Close to this dark grotto,
Where the air is so soft,
The water contends with pebbles,
And light contends with shade.

In this form the return of the *a* rhyme is suspended, giving the fourth line of the stanza a dose of added drama, and perhaps contributing to a sense that the *b* lines are in parentheses. The second part of the stanza is also a mirror image of the first part, the original *ab* pattern turned back upon itself into *ba*.

These features may give the *abba* pattern a greater unity and symmetry, not to say self-absorption, than its *abab* counterpart. Certainly, the form would seem to add to the sense of enclosure in L'Hermite's dark grotto, as well as complementing, by its mirror form, the references later in the poem to Narcissus.

What would be the impact if a poet switched between the two schemes in the same poem? An interesting example is provided by Fauré's "Les berceaux," where the rimes croisées of the first two stanzas give way in the final stanza to rimes embrassées.

Le long du quai les grands vaisseaux,   *a*
Que la houle incline en silence,   *b*
Ne prennent pas garde aux berceaux   *a*
Que la main des femmes balance.   *b*

Mais viendra le jour des adieux,   *c*
Car il faut que les femmes pleurent,   *d*
Et que les hommes curieux   *c*
Tentent les horizons qui leurrent.   *d*

Et ce jour-là les grands vaisseaux,	*a*
Fuyant le port qui diminue,	*e*
Sentent leur masse retenue	*e*
Par l'âme des lointains berceaux.[5]	*a*

Along the quay the great ships,
Listing silently with the surge,
Pay no heed to the cradles
Rocked by the women's hands.

But the day of parting will come,
For it is decreed that women shall weep,
And that men with questing spirits
Shall seek enticing horizons.

And on that day the great ships,
Leaving the dwindling harbour behind,
Shall feel their hulls held back
By the soul of the distant cradles.

There are several effects:

- First, the change in the rhyme scheme extends the physical distance between the two words that are at the heart of the poem — "vaisseaux" and "berceaux." One can almost see the ships sailing away within the very layout of the third stanza of the verse.
- On the other hand, the rapid return of the middle rhyme within this stanza ("diminue"/"retenue") hints that the ships are not going to escape so easily after all, that the bonds are tighter than expected.
- Finally, would it be fanciful to suggest that the change in rhyme scheme contributes to a broadening of theme within the third stanza — that this is not, in the end, a straightforward narrative about ships leaving port, but a more profound and dramatic statement about separation and loss?

OTHER STANZAIC FORMS

The couplet and the quatrain are probably the most common ways of organizing lines of French verse. However, a variety of other patterns exist, many of which contain couplets or quatrains within their structures.

THE SIZAIN

The "sizain," or 6-line stanza, has a long history in French poetry.

The most common rhyme scheme for the sizain during the sixteenth to nineteenth centuries was *aabccb* (sometimes referred to as the "minor ode stanza"). Verlaine's "Chanson d'automne," set by Hahn, is an example:

Les sanglots longs	*a*
Des violons	*a*
De l'automne	*b*
Blessent mon cœur	*c*
D'une langueur	*c*
Monotone.	*b*

With long sobs
The violins
   Of autumn
Wound my heart
With languorous
   Monotony.

Other forms of the sizain also exist. Hahn's song "Infidélité," based on Gautier's poem of the same name, has an *abbacc* pattern, while his setting of Banville's "L'enamourée" uses sizains with an *ababcc* rhyme scheme.

All three of these examples combine a couplet with a quatrain either in rimes embrassées or rimes croisées. However, the internal organization of the stanza may cut across these subdivisions. In the Verlaine example above, for instance, the syntax tends to divide the stanza down the middle, creating a pattern perhaps best described as *aab/ccb*.

THE DIZAIN

The "dizain," or 10-line stanza, offers many potential variations. Perhaps the most common form, sometimes called the "major ode stanza," has a rhyme scheme *ababccdeed*. Passerat's "Ode du premier jour de mai," set by Gounod, is an example.

Laissons le lit et le sommeil	*a*
Cette journée:	*b*
Pour nous l'Aurore au front vermeil	*a*
Est déjà née.	*b*
Or que le ciel est le plus gai	*c*
En ce gracieux mois de mai,	*c*
Aimons, mignonne;	*d*
Contentons notre ardent désir:	*e*
En ce monde n'a du plaisir	*e*
Qui ne s'en donne.	*d*

Let us leave our beds and throw off sleep
    On this day,
For us the crimson dawn
    Has already broken.
Now the sky is at its brightest
In this kindly month of May,
    Let us love, my sweet!
Let us slake our ardent desire,
There's no pleasure in this world
    For those who do not yield to it.

In this variation, the dizain combines a forward-moving quatrain in rimes croisées with a couplet that suspends movement and acts as a fulcrum for the poem and an inward-looking final quatrain in rimes embrassées. Although its punctuation to some extent cuts across these internal divisions, the stanza above does follow this general pattern—an energetic wake-up call is followed by an explanation of the poet's joy (this is Spring in all its glory), which then leads into the more serious theme of the poem, that time passes and we must seize the day.

Other forms of the dizain include the variation *abbacdcdee*. A famous instance is Duparc's setting of Gautier's "Au pays où se fait la guerre." The poet here uses the final couplet of each stanza as a refrain, underlining not only the crushing loneliness of the woman left behind by her lover, but also her relentless brooding on her fate.

THE TERCET

The "tercet," or 3-line stanza, is relatively uncommon in French verse and in the mélodie.

One of its most famous forms, the "terza rima" of Dante's *Divine Comedy*, was tried in French verse in the sixteenth century and then more or less abandoned until the nineteenth century, when it was taken up once again by poets such as Leconte de Lisle.

In this form of tercet, the middle rhyme of the first stanza becomes the rhyme for lines 1 and 3 of the following stanza, creating a pattern *aba bcb cdc* etc. The pattern is closed by a single line that rhymes with the middle line of the previous group: *yzy z*. This constant interlinking of stanzas gives the terza rima a powerful forward movement.

A rare example of the use of terza rima in the mélodie can be found in Verlaine's poem "J'allais par des chemins perfides," set by Fauré.

J'allais par des chemins perfides,	*a*
Douloureusement incertain.	*b*
Vos chères mains furent mes guides.	*a*
Si pâle à l'horizon lointain	*b*
Luisait un faible espoir d'aurore;	*c*
Votre regard fut le matin.	*b*

I walked along treacherous ways,
Painfully uncertain.
Your dear hands guided me.

So pale on the far horizon
A faint hope of dawn was gleaming;
Your gaze was the morning.

The song "N'est-ce pas?" from the same cycle of Verlaine settings, also uses terza rima. However, here Fauré leaves out several verses of the original poem, thereby completely disrupting the rhyme scheme— a warning for poetry enthusiasts that the rules of verse are sometimes suspended in the mélodie!

Another form of tercet is the "tercet monorime," where the same rhyme is repeated throughout each stanza, giving a rhyme scheme *aaa bbb ccc* etc. Although this form appears in early French verse, it is perhaps best known through its use by poets in the late nineteenth century, particularly the Symbolists, who exploited its qualities of incantation to suggest states of almost haunted spiritual impotence and ennui. Cros's "Nocturne," set by Chausson as "Chanson perpétuelle," offers an example.

Puisque je n'ai plus mon ami,	*a*
Je mourrai dans l'étang, parmi	*a*
Les fleurs, sous le flot endormi.	*a*

Since I no longer have my lover,
I shall die in the pool among
The flowers beneath the still water.

THE QUINTIL

The "quintil" or 5-line stanza has a long history in French verse but is found infrequently in the mélodie. Apollinaire adopted an *ababa* form of the stanza in the early twentieth century that appears in some mélodies, such as Poulenc's setting of "1904."

À Strasbourg en 1904	*a*
J'arrivai pour le lundi gras	*b*
À l'hôtel m'assis devant l'âtre	*a*
Près d'un chanteur de l'Opéra	*b*
Qui ne parlait que de théâtre	*a*

In Strasbourg in 1904
I arrived for Shrove Monday
At the hotel sat down by the fireside
Next to a singer from the Opéra
Who spoke only of theatre

The effect can be likened to that of a quatrain in rimes croisées thrown forward one more pace, ending the stanza in a slightly awkward or uneasy mode.

THE SEPTAIN

The "septain" or 7-line stanza makes occasional appearances in the mélodie. An example is Saint-Saëns's "L'attente" (a setting of Hugo's poem "Attente"), which has an *aabcccb* rhyme scheme.

Monte, écureuil, monte au grand chêne,	*a*
Sur la branche des cieux prochaine,	*a*
Qui plie et tremble comme un jonc.	*b*
Cigogne, aux vieilles tours fidèle,	*c*
Oh! vole et monte à tire-d'aile	*c*
De l'église à la citadelle,	*c*
Du haut clocher au grand donjon.	*b*

Squirrel, ascend the towering oak,
To the branch right next to the sky

Bending and trembling like a reed.
Stork, faithful to the ancient towers,
Swiftly ascend and wing your way
From the church to the citadel,
From the lofty steeple to the mighty keep.

THE HUITAIN

Victor Hugo is the source of several examples of 8-line stanzas or "huitains." Saint-Saëns's setting of "Le pas d'armes du roi Jean" follows this pattern, with its *ababcccb* rhyme scheme:

Par saint-Gille,	*a*
Viens-nous-en,	*b*
Mon agile	*a*
Alezan;	*b*
Viens, écoute,	*c*
Par la route,	*c*
Voir la joute	*c*
Du roi Jean.	*b*

By Saint Giles,
Let us set out,
My nimble
Chestnut steed;
Come, hear me:
We're off
To see King John's
Jousting contest.

Berlioz's "La captive," another setting of a poem by Hugo, follows the same scheme.

SOME FINAL THOUGHTS ON STANZAS

It is impossible in a short guide such as this to do justice to the variety of stanzaic forms and rhyme schemes found in the mélodie. Moreover, we can only touch briefly on some of the other elements in a poem that may create complementary or countervailing patterns within an overall stanzaic structure.

We have already seen, in Verlaine's "Chanson d'automne," how syntax can cut across a stanza's rhyme scheme. Punctuation and typographical layout can also be exploited for expressive effect. In Verlaine's "La lune blanche," for example, the last line of each sizain is separated from the rest of the stanza by a set of dots and a blank line, creating a pattern that might be notated as *ababc/c*.

La lune blanche	*a*
Luit dans les bois;	*b*
De chaque branche	*a*
Part une voix	*b*
Sous la ramée...	*c*
Ô bien-aimée.	*c*

The white moon
Gleams in the woods;
From every branch
There comes a voice
Beneath the boughs...

O my beloved.

This structure helps to suggest the poet's leap into amorous reverie, while at the same time the second *c* rhyme (and particularly its return as part of a couplet) underscores the close link between this reverie and the description of nature in the main part of the stanza.

A different effect is created by the punctuation and typography in Verlaine's "Spleen," set by Debussy. Here, the division into isolated two-line segments of what would normally be quatrains in rimes croisées helps to engender a sense of structural dislocation in the poem that seems entirely appropriate to its content.

Les roses étaient toutes rouges,	*a*
Et les lierres étaient tout noirs.	*b*
Chère, pour peu que tu te bouges,	*a*
Renaissent tous mes désespoirs.	*b*

All the roses were red
And the ivy was all black.

Dear, at your slightest move
All my despair revives.

Poets may also use variations in meter to create patterns within their poems. In Baudelaire's "L'invitation au voyage," the disposition of 5- and 7-syllable lines mirrors the rhyme scheme of the poem, contributing to the sense of "luxe, calme et volupté."

Mon enfant, ma sœur,	*a*
Songe à la douceur	*a*
D'aller là-bas vivre ensemble!	*b*
Aimer à loisir,	*c*
Aimer et mourir	*c*
Au pays qui te ressemble!	*b*

My child, my sister,
Think how sweet
To journey there and live together!
To love as we please,

To love and die
In the land that is like you!

By way of contrast, in Verlaine's poem "L'ombre des arbres dans la rivière embrumée," set by Debussy and Hahn, rhyming 12- and 7-syllable lines immediately follow one another, giving a sense that the potential expansiveness and weightiness of the longer line is constantly being brought back to dismal reality by its shorter and more incisive partner.

| L'ombre des arbres dans la rivière embrumée | *a* |
| Meurt comme de la fumée | *a* |

The shadow of trees in the misty stream
Dies like smoke

Both the Baudelaire and Verlaine examples above illustrate changes of meter within stanzas; but, of course, poets can create variations between stanzas as well. Baudelaire's poem "Le jet d'eau," set by Debussy, uses octosyllables in the main stanzas, but the refrain is a mixture of 4- and 6-syllable lines, helping to vary the pace and tone of the poem.

5 ✑ Sonnets, Rondels, and Other Fixed Forms

*F*RENCH POETS, like their English counterparts, have a range of traditional verse templates or "fixed forms" upon which they can draw. Students of the mélodie will inevitably come across settings based on them.

In this chapter, I examine four of the main fixed forms: the sonnet, rondel, villanelle, and ballade. In each case, I set out the form's basic structure, including any important variations, before discussing its key features.

THE SONNET

The sonnet made its first appearance in French verse during the sixteenth century, and, apart from a period in the eighteenth century when it fell out of favor, has been a fixture of the poetic landscape ever since.

The French sonnet is more directly linked to its Italian forbears than its English equivalent.[1] Its 14 lines traditionally have a rhyme scheme *abba abba ccd ede* (although *ccd eed* is also an accepted standard pattern for the final six lines). In this guise, the sonnet therefore combines a pair of quatrains, based on only two rhymes and organized in *rimes embrassées*, with a pair of tercets using three rhymes. Unlike the English sonnet, the four stanzas are traditionally separated typographically. Mallarmé's poem "Surgi de la croupe et du bond," set by Ravel, is an example of the classic form.[2]

Surgi de la croupe et du bond   *a*
D'une verrerie éphémère   *b*
Sans fleurir la veillée amère   *b*
Le col ignoré s'interrompt.   *a*

Je crois bien que deux bouches n'ont   *a*
Bu, ni son amant ni ma mère,   *b*
Jamais à la même Chimère,   *b*
Moi, sylphe de ce froid plafond!   *a*

Le pur vase d'aucun breuvage   *c*
Que l'inexhaustible veuvage   *c*
Agonise mais ne consent,   *d*

Naïf baiser des plus funèbres!   *e*
À rien expirer annonçant   *d*
Une rose dans les ténèbres.   *e*

Risen from the crupper and leap
Of an ephemeral ornament of glass,
Without garlanding the bitter vigil,
The neglected neck stops short.

I truly believe that two mouths never
Drank, neither her lover nor my mother,
From the same Chimera,
I, sylph of this cold ceiling!

The vase pure of any draught
Save inexhaustible widowhood
Though dying does not consent—

Naïve and most funereal kiss—
To breathe forth any annunciation
Of a rose in the shadows.

Duparc's setting of Robert de Bonnières's "Le manoir de Rosemonde" offers an example of the alternative *ccd eed* arrangement of the tercets.[3]

En passant par où j'ai passé	c
Tu verras que seul et blessé	c
J'ai parcouru ce triste monde.	d
Et qu'ainsi je m'en fus mourir	e
Bien loin, bien loin, sans découvrir	e
Le bleu manoir de Rosemonde.	d

Passing by where I have passed,
You will see that, solitary and wounded,
I have traversed this sorry world,

And that thus I went off to die
Far, far away, without ever finding
The blue manor of Rosamonde.

Such is the poetic energy that has been invested in the sonnet over time, however, that variants to these traditional forms abound. Examples include:

- The use of rimes croisées rather than rimes embrassées in the quatrains. Chausson's "Le colibri," for instance, has a rhyme scheme *abab abab ccd ede*.
- The introduction of a second set of rhymes in the second quatrain. In Leconte de Lisle's "Le parfum impérissable," set by Fauré, the rhyme scheme for the quatrains is *abab cdcd*.
- The combination of rimes croisées and rimes embrassées in the quatrains. Félix Arvers's poem "Sonnet," set by Bizet as "Ma vie a son secret," has an *abab baab* rhyme scheme for the first eight lines.

Other arrangements are possible. Baudelaire's sonnet "La vie antérieure," set by Duparc, maintains a pattern of rimes embrassées in the quatrains but switches the rhymes to create the pattern *abba baab*. This poem also has an unusual *cdd cee* rhyme scheme in the tercets.

Sonnets are highly complex. Unlike some of the other fixed forms we explore below, they make no use of refrains, so the poet is able to — indeed, expected to — develop his or her ideas continuously, but within very tight formal constraints.

The division of the French sonnet into separate stanzas encourages the reader to make comparisons between the two quatrains and between the two tercets; meanwhile, the move from the relatively static and deliberate quatrains, with their solid enclosed rhymes, to the more volatile tercets (each of which is structurally incomplete) is, most commentators agree, a key dramatic moment in a sonnet. The poet Louis Aragon, in his essay *Du sonnet*, speaks of the "corset étroit des quatrains," contrasting this with "cette évasion de l'esprit, cette liberté raisonable du rêve, des tercets."

As Aragon's comments suggest, the structural shift from the quatrains to the tercets within a sonnet often coincides with a movement in meaning and tone, in what is commonly referred to as the "volta" or "turn." Typically, the poem turns from description to reverie, from exposition to analysis, or from experience to emotion as the poet develops, clarifies, or reveals the true significance of what has gone before and builds up to the concluding line.

The ninth line in Baudelaire's "La vie antérieure," for example, begins an emotional exploration of the lost world described in the preceding quatrains, which leads ultimately to the identification of the enigmatic "secret douloureux" at the heart of the poet's experience.

C'est là que j'ai vécu dans les voluptés calmes[4]

It is there that I have lived in sensuous repose

However, the volta does not invariably appear at line 9, as is illustrated by mélodies such as Chausson's "La caravane," a setting of Gautier's sonnet of the same name, where the examination of the true significance of the metaphor upon which the poem is based begins at the twelfth line, that is, at the beginning of the second tercet:

> Dieu, pour vous reposer, dans le désert du temps,
> Comme des oasis, a mis les cimetières;
> Couchez-vous et dormez, voyageurs haletants.

> God, to offer you rest, in the desert of time
> Has placed, like oases, cemeteries;
> Breathless travellers, lie down and sleep.

THE RONDEL

The rondel is one of a number of forms originally associated with dance rounds that found renewed favor in the latter half of the nineteenth century, in large part through the efforts of Théodore de Banville.

The basic shape of the rondel is *ABba abAB abbaA*; the capital letters indicate lines that repeat in the poem, and the lower case letters identify the rhyme scheme (as usual). This is the form found in Charles d'Orléans's "Quand je fus pris au pavillon," set by Hahn.

Quand je fus pris au pavillon	*A*
De ma dame, très gente et belle,	*B*
Je me brûlay à la chandelle,	*b*
Ainsi que fait le papillon.	*a*
Je rougis comme vermillon,	*a*
À la clarté d'une étincelle,	*b*
Quand je fus pris au pavillon	*A*
De ma dame, très gente et belle.	*B*
Si j'eusse été esmerillon	*a*
Ou que j'eusse eu aussi bonne aile,	*b*
Je me fusse gardé de celle	*b*

Qui me bailla de l'auguillon,   *a*

Quand je fus pris au pavillon.   A

When I was caught in the pavilion
Of my most beautiful and noble lady,
I burnt myself in the candle's flame,
As the moth does.

I flushed crimson
In the brightness of a spark,
When I was caught in the pavilion
Of my most beautiful and noble lady.

If I had been a merlin
Or had wings as strong,
I should have shielded myself
From her who pierced me with her arrows,
When I was caught in the pavilion.

The rondel therefore makes significant technical demands on the poet, who needs to find five *a* rhymes and five *b* rhymes. A certain virtuosity is also required to ensure that the refrains are not mere repetition for its own sake but that they illuminate a new aspect of the original idea each time.

In expert hands, however, the very constraints of the form can bestow on the rondel a strong musical and thematic unity, making it highly expressive. In Charles d'Orléans's "Pour ce que Plaisance est morte" (set by Debussy), for example, the constant return to the opening line lends the poem an immobility and haunting insistence — truly the poet cannot break out of the cycle of despair.

Pour ce que Plaisance est morte
Ce may, suis vestu de noir

Because Plaisance is dead
This May, I am attired in black

By way of contrast, in Koechlin's setting of Banville's rondel "Le thé," the refrain is an important part of the joke, suggesting how the poet is repeatedly pulled back from his musings on the violent and erotic images on the Chinese crockery (reveries that presumably reflect his longings for Miss Ellen) to the niceties of the social setting in which he finds himself.

Là sous un ciel rouge irrité,	*a*
Une dame fière et sournoise	*b*
Montre en ses longs yeux de turquoise	*b*
L'extase et la naïveté:	*a*
Miss Ellen, versez-moi le Thé.	*A*

There, beneath an angry red sky,
A lady, proud and sly,
Reveals in her wide turquoise eyes
Ecstasy and innocence:
Miss Ellen, pour me tea.

Two other aspects of the rondel are worth noting. First, there is often a change of tone after the second stanza, rather like the volta in the sonnet. So in Banville's "Le printemps," set by Hahn, the beautiful season of the first two stanzas becomes, in the third, the healer of all ills and the generator of a multitude of hopes in humankind.

Mille espoirs fabuleux nourrissent
Nos cœurs émus et palpitants.

A thousand fabled hopes nourish
Our full and beating hearts.

Similarly, in the same composer's "Les étoiles," again a setting of Banville, a relatively measured description of the heavens is transformed, in the final five lines, into an ecstatic vision of cosmic beauty.

Quel peintre mettra sur ses toiles,	*a*
Ô Dieu! leurs clairs fourmillements,	*b*
Ces fournaises de diamants	*b*
Qu'à nos yeux ravis tu dévoiles,	*a*
Les cieux resplendissants d'Étoiles?	*A*

What painter will capture on canvas,
O God, this limpid teeming,
These diamantine furnaces
You unveil to our enraptured eyes,
The heavens resplendent with Stars?

Second, the disappearance of the latter part of the refrain in the third stanza of the rondel focuses particular attention on its last line, leaving the reader in a state of heightened expectation and evoking what one critic has called a "vision qui s'éternise."[5] Charles d'Orléans's "Pour ce que Plaisance est morte" again provides an example, the stark and poignant last line inviting us to ponder not just the personal tragedy of Plaisance's death but also its significance to all Nature, of which the final stanza has spoken.

THE VILLANELLE

The English villanelle is a true fixed form, based on a set number of lines (traditionally nineteen, as in poems such as Dylan Thomas's "Do not go gentle into that good night"), two rhymes and two refrains. French poets have treated the villanelle more flexibly since its first appearance in French verse in the sixteenth century, expanding or contracting the number of lines at will, although maintaining the pattern of two rhymes and two refrains.[6]

Sonnets, Rondels, and Other Fixed Forms

The six villanelles that make up Honegger's *Saluste du Bartas* sequence, using texts by Pierre Bédat de Monlaur, are examples of a compact 13-line variant used also by poets such as Leconte de Lisle. The structure of each poem is A1 *b* A2 / *a b* A1 / *a b* A2 / *a b* A1 A2, where the numbered capital letters denote refrain lines. The first poem, "Le château du Bartas," illustrates the form.

Un Gascon à mine fière	A1
Écrit de beaux vers pompeux	*b*
Dans cette gentilhommière.	A2
Il ressemble comme un frère	*a*
À Monluc, illustre preux,	*b*
Un Gascon à mine fière.	A1
Le jeune poète espère	*a*
Un jour revenir fameux	*b*
Dans cette gentilhommière.	A2
Gloire! Descends sur la terre	*a*
Èlire au dessus des dieux	*b*
Un Gascon à mine fière	A1
Dans cette gentilhommière.	A2

A Gascon of proud mien
Writes beautiful high-flown poesy
In this country-seat.

He could be taken for a brother
Of Monluc, that illustrious knight,
A Gascon of proud mien.

The young poet hopes
To return famous one day
To this country-seat.

49

O Glory! Descend to earth
And elevate above the gods
A Gascon of proud mien
In this country-seat.

Rosemonde Gérard's "Villanelle des petits canards" (set by Chabrier), on the other hand, is an example of a looser form of villanelle that could, in theory, continue indefinitely. Here the structure is *A1 b A2 / a b A1 / a b A2 / a b A1 / a b A2 . . . a b A1 A2*, where the ellipses indicate that the poet can insert however many stanzas he or she wishes.

Ils vont, les petits canards,	*A1*
Tout au bord de la rivière,	*b*
Comme de bons campagnards!	*A2*
Barboteurs et frétillards,	*a*
Heureux de troubler l'eau claire,	*b*
Ils vont, les petits canards.	*A1*
Ils semblent un peu jobards,	*a*
Mais ils sont à leur affaire,	*b*
Comme de bons campagnards!	*A2*

There they go, the little ducks,
All along the river bank,
Like good country-folk!

Paddling and waggling,
Happy to muddy the clear water,
They go on their way, the little ducks,

A little gullible, perhaps,
But they go about their business,
Like good country-folk!

The technical challenges of the villanelle are similar to those of the rondel, in particular the need to create variety within the overall unity and insistence of the form. The poet must find interesting rhyme words within the limited two-rhyme scheme and vary the entrance of the refrains so that they add something new to the poem each time.

Note also that the two final lines of the poem place the two refrains side by side for the first time. Some critics have suggested that the villanelle oscillates between two different states that are finally reconciled at the end of the poem.[7] Such a case could certainly be made for the "Villanelle des petits canards," where the clearly duck-like activities of stanzas 2, 4, and 6 and the more human characteristics described in stanzas 3, 5, and 7 begin to blur in stanzas 8 and 9, leaving the final stanza 10 to suggest how little there is to distinguish the ducks and the country-folk in their amorous ambling.

Amoureux et nasillards,	*a*
Chacun avec sa commère,	*b*
Ils vont, les petits canards,	*A1*
Comme de bons campagnards!	*A2*

Amorous and snuffling,
Each one with his lady,
They go on their way, the little ducks,
Like good country-folk!

THE BALLADE

The ballade form, which dates back to the fourteenth century, makes an occasional appearance in the mélodie. It has a number of major variants.[8]

The "ballade primitive" is built around 8-line stanzas, typically with an *ababbccB* rhyme scheme, where *B* is a refrain that repeats throughout the poem. In its basic form, the number of stanzas is infinite, although the fact that the ballade primitive has only three rhymes provides a practical limit. Chabrier's setting of Rostand's "Ballade des gros dindons," with its four stanzas, is an example (although the rhyme scheme is more typical of the petite ballade form discussed below).

The "petite ballade" is nowadays primarily associated with the poet François Villon. Unlike the ballade primitive, the petite ballade is a true fixed form with a set number of lines, typically twenty-eight, distributed in three 8-line stanzas with an *ababbcbC* rhyme scheme (where C is a refrain), followed by a 4-line "envoi" with a *bcbC* rhyme scheme in which the poet directly addresses a personage of high rank in order to draw a message from the poem and to provide a conclusion. The third stanza and envoi from Villon's "Ballade des femmes de Paris," set by Debussy, provide a good example of the structure.

Brettes, Suysses, n'y sçavent guères,	*a*
Ne Gasconnes et Tholouzaines;	*b*
Du Petit Pont deux harangères	*a*
Les concluront, et les Lorraines,	*b*
Anglesches ou Callaisiennes,	*b*
(Ay-je beaucoup de lieux compris?)	*c*
Picardes, de Valenciennes . . .	*b*
Il n'est bon bec que de Paris.	*C*
Prince, aux dames parisiennes,	*b*
De bien parler donner le prix;	*c*
Quoy qu'on dit d'Italiennes,	*b*
Il n'est bon bec que de Paris.	*C*

Bretons and Swiss are mere beginners,
Like Gascons and Toulousains;
Two jabberers on the Petit Pont
Would silence them and Lorrainers too,
And women from England and from Calais
(I've named a lot of places, eh?),

From Picardy and Valencienne . . .
There's no tongue like a Parisian one.

Prince, to the ladies of Paris
Present the prize for fine chatter;
Whatever is said of Italians,
There's no tongue like a Parisian one.

Finally, there is the "grande ballade," which typically has three 10-line stanzas, each with a rhyme scheme *ababbccdcD* (where *D* is a refrain) and a 5-line envoi in a *ccdcD* pattern, making thirty-five lines in total. The stanzas of Villon's "Ballade pour prier Nostre Dame," also set by Debussy, follow the grande ballade model, although the composer omits the unusual 7-line envoi in the original poem.

Dame du ciel, régente terrienne,	*a*
Emperière des infernaulx paluz,	*b*
Recevez-moy, vostre humble chrestienne,	*a*
Que comprinse soye entre vos esleuz,	*b*
Ce non obstant qu'oncques riens ne valuz.	*b*
Les biens de vous, ma dame et ma maistresse,	*c*
Sont trop plus grans que ne suys pecheresse,	*c*
Sans lesquelz bien ame ne peult merir	*d*
N'avoir les cieulx, je n'en suis menteresse.	*c*
En ceste foy je vueil vivre et mourir.	*D*

Lady of Heaven, Regent of earth,
Empress of the infernal swamps,
Take me, your humble Christian,
To be numbered among your elect,
Though my worth has been as nothing.
Your mercy, my Lady and my Mistress,
Is much greater than my sinfulness,
Without it no soul can merit

Nor enter Heaven, I do not lie.
In this faith I wish to live and die.

The technical challenges of the ballade form are great. For instance, the poet has to find fourteen different *b* rhymes in the petite ballade and twelve different *c* rhymes in the grande ballade. In the view of some commentators,[9] the constraints of the rhyme scheme lend the ballade, like the rondel, a particular thematic and musical unity, while its refrain brings us constantly back to the heart of the poem. Both of these Villon ballades would seem to support these contentions. Meanwhile, the short envoi, which again repeats the refrain, is a particularly effective way of bringing out the main message of the poem and drawing it to a close.

6 ✣ Rhyme

IN CHAPTER 4 we saw the importance of rhyme in delineating stanzas. In this chapter, I examine rhyme in more detail, as an element of verse in its own right.[1] I then explore briefly the wider sound patterns that poets create in their works.

THE ESSENCE OF FRENCH VERSE?

From medieval times until the end of the nineteenth century, rhyme was considered an essential—indeed, *the* essential—feature of French lyric poetry. Unlike its English counterpart, French poetry does not have a blank verse tradition, nor are rhyme schemes such as *xaxa*—where *x* represents an unrhymed line—common, as they are in English.

Nineteenth century texts on French verse constantly underline the importance of rhyme. In his *Petit traité de poésie française*, published in 1872,[2] the poet Théodore de Banville claimed "la RIME . . . est l'unique harmonie des vers et elle est tout le vers . . . *l'imagination de la Rime* est, entre toutes, la qualité qui constitue le poëte." For the classicist and verse theorist Louis Quicherat, "la rime est le fondement et la condition de notre poésie."[3]

Rhyme's perceived indispensability was based on a number of claims:

- Rhyme helps to differentiate verse from prose. In a language where accent is relatively weak and different meters are determined by syllable count, rhyme is essential to mark the end of lines and to help the listener identify the prevailing verse form(s). Without rhyme, verse would become indistinguishable from prose.

- Rhyme generates thought, creating its own levels of meaning in verse by linking words in surprising ways. In Banville's view, the ideal rhyme combined the greatest similarity of sound with the greatest difference in meaning. Many of the poets of the late nineteenth century, such as the Symbolists, regarded rhyming as a semi-mystical activity and felt that the correspondences of ideas created by rhyme were profound.
- Rhyme is a key element in the music of verse. By linking sounds in harmonious ways, and by generating cycles of aural expectation and fulfilment for the listener, rhyme delights the ear as well as the mind. It also helps to create patterns of intonation within a poem, the rhyme at the end of each line acting as a point of destination for the reader.

Some of these ideas did not survive into the twentieth century—free verse poets, for instance, would view rhythm, not rhyme, as the essence of verse, as we shall see. Nevertheless, rhyme remains a fundamental concern for many of the poets of the mélodie.

WHAT IS RHYME IN FRENCH?

Rhyme in regular French verse is based primarily on identity of sound rather than of spelling. The core of any rhyme is the vowel; the minimum condition is that the stressed or "tonic" vowel in both rhyme-words should be identical phonetically.[4] Régnier's poem "Chanson," set by Fauré, offers an example of the most basic rhyme.

> Il n'est de fleuve attendu
>
> . . . .
> . . . .
> De la source où tu as bu
>
> I await no river
>
> . . . .
> . . . .
> From the spring where you have drunk.

Like English, however, French versification makes a distinction between rhyme and assonance. In essence, where consonants are sounded after the tonic vowel, as in the example below taken from Baudelaire's "Les hiboux" (set by Séverac), those consonants must also be identical phonetically if rhyme is to exist.

> Leur attitude au sage ens**eigne**
> Qu'il faut en ce monde qu'il cr**aigne**

> From their pose the wise man learns
> That in this world he ought to fear

If the consonants sounded after the tonic vowel are different, then assonance, not rhyme, is created. So "vitre" (window-pane) rhymes with "epître" (epistle), but the relationship of both words to "Chypre" (Cyprus) is one of assonance. Assonance was used extensively in early French poetry and later reappeared as an important element in free verse, as we shall see in Chapter 7.

This guide is not the place to explore further the sounds of the French language. Any good dictionary will give the phonetic transcription of specific words.[5] For the purposes of analyzing verse, however, we do need to consider in more detail two aspects of French poetic practice: "rhyme degree" and "rhyme gender."

RHYME DEGREE

By the nineteenth century, poets and verse theorists had developed an elaborate system of analysis that classified rhymes by degree.[6] The main categories were as follows:

- "rime pauvre" (or "faible"): where only the tonic vowel rhymes—for instance, v**ie**/fol**ie**
- "rime suffisante": where the tonic vowel and any following consonant(s) rhyme—for instance, b**elle**/immort**elle**
- "rime riche": where the tonic vowel, any following consonant(s),

and any immediately preceding consonant(s) (known technically
as the "consonne(s) d'appui") rhyme—for instance, **passe**/**espace**
or b**rises**/**grises**

- "rime léonine": where the tonic vowel, any following consonant(s),
any immediately preceding consonant(s) and any immediately pre-
ceding vowel(s) rhyme—for instance, br**euvage**/**veuvage**

This system was by no means perfect and threw up some oddities.
For instance, the second stanza of Hugo's "Dans les ruines d'une
abbaye," set by Fauré, runs:

> Quels rires étincelants
> Dans ces ombres
> Jadis pleines de front blancs,
> De coeurs sombres!

> What sparkling laughter
> In these shadows
> Once full of pale faces
> And sombre hearts!

Under the above rules the rhyme "étincelants"/"blancs" would be
classified as riche, because of the existence of a common "consonne
d'appui," whereas the rhyme "ombres"/"sombres" is merely suffisante,
despite its much denser concentration of sounds. During the twentieth
century, therefore, a simpler system of classification was adopted, based
on the number of identical elements in the rhyming words.[7] However,
any student of the mélodie should be aware of the traditional system.

Being able to distinguish the different types of rhyme is valuable, as
rhyme degree may have an expressive function within a poem. Rime
riche, for instance, can be used deliberately to suggest fullness or abun-
dance as well as to highlight the poet's own dexterity.[8] The sequence of
such rhymes in Debussy's setting of Banville's "Pierrot" helps not only
to emphasize the extraordinary nature of the scene, but also to under-
line the poet's playfulness and enjoyment of language.

Le bon Pierrot, que la foule contemple,
Ayant fini les noces d'Arlequin,
Suit en songeant le boulevard du Temple.
Une fillette au souple casaquin
En vain l'agace de son oeil coquin;
Et cependant mystérieuse et lisse
Faisant de lui sa plus chère délice,
La blanche Lune aux cornes de taureaux
Jette un regard de son oeil en coulisse
À son ami Jean Gaspard Deburau.

Good old Pierrot, watched by the crowd,
Having done with Harlequin's wedding,
Drifts dreamily along the boulevard du Temple.
A girl in a flowing blouse
Vainly leads him on with her teasing eyes;
And meanwhile, mysterious and sleek,
Cherishing him above all else,
The white moon with horns like a bull
Ogles her friend
Jean Gaspard Deburau.

Rimes pauvres or suffisantes, on the other hand, may conjure up the prosaic, the uninspired, the weary. It is no surprise to find that the rhymes in poems such as Verlaine's "Le ciel est, par-dessus le toit" (set by Fauré and Hahn) and his "Il pleure dans mon cœur" (set by Debussy) are predominantly of this type, as if the poet lacks the energy and will to attempt anything more elaborate.[9]

Meanwhile, the contrast between rhymes of different degree may be used structurally within a poem to draw the reader or listener's attention to moments of heightened significance. It seems fitting, for example, that Leconte de Lisle's "Phidylé"—already a very rich text acoustically—should culminate in a stanza with two rimes léonines, the erotic charge of these final lines matched by the plenitude of their rhymes.

Mais quand l'Astre, incliné sur sa courbe éclatante,
　　Verra ses ardeurs s'apaiser,
Que ton plus beau sourire et ton meilleur baiser
　　Me récompensent de l'attente!

But when the sun, low on its dazzling curve,
　　Sees its brilliance wane,
Let your loveliest smile and finest kiss
　　Reward me for my waiting!

RHYME GENDER

French versification makes a distinction between "masculine" and "feminine" rhymes. Masculine rhymes are based on words where the main stress falls on the final syllable: "dé**serts**"/"**airs**," "hori**zon**"/ "ga**zon**," "cr**eux**"/"y**eux**," "révé**ler**"/"rappe**ler**," to take some examples from Lamartine's poem "Le soir," set by Gounod. In feminine rhymes, the syllable bearing the main stress is followed by a mute e: "si**lence**"/ "s'a**vance**," "noc**turne**"/"taci**turne**," "mys**tère**"/"s**phère**" and so on from the same poem. Note that rhyme gender has nothing to do with the gender of the word itself. Words such as "beauté" and "mer" are feminine nouns but form masculine rhymes.[10]

The concept of rhyme gender is not unique to French. English versification also has masculine rhymes, such as "dress"/"press," where the stress falls on the final syllable, and feminine rhymes, such as "ocean"/"devotion," where the stress falls on the penultimate syllable.[11] However, as is the case with rhyme degree, this categorization is not part of a wider system in English, and the extensive use of feminine rhymes often sounds false or intrusive.

In regular French verse, on the other hand, rhyme gender is a subject of real significance. Two issues, in particular, are much discussed.

The rules set out above dictate that many masculine rhymes will end with a vowel sound. The second and fourth lines of Apollinaire's "L'écrevisse," set by Poulenc, offer an example:

> . . . .
> Vous et moi nous nous en allons
> . . . .
> À reculons, à reculons.

In contrast, the last sound heard in most feminine rhymes will be a consonant, as the other two lines of Apollinaire's short poem demonstrate:

> Incertitude, Ô mes délices
> . . . .
> Comme s'en vont les écrevisses,
> . . . .

> Uncertainty, O! my delights
> You and I we progress
> As crayfish progress,
> Backwards, backwards.

The presence of a mute e on feminine rhymes, even if not articulated, has traditionally been thought to have an impact on the pronuciation of the rhyme word, prolonging the tonic vowel and any following consonants and creating a lingering or echoing effect.

A sort of literary sexism therefore runs through much traditional thinking about French verse, with masculine rhymes being perceived as abrupt, hard, and unyielding, while feminine rhymes are seen as softer, gentler, and more evanescent.

Understanding French Verse

By the end of the sixteenth century, it had become widely accepted practice for masculine and feminine rhymes to alternate within a French poem. At each change of rhyme, the rhyme gender would also change. The first two stanzas of Musset's "Venise," set by Gounod, are an example:

Dans Venise la rouge,	*a* (feminine)
Pas un bateau qui bouge,	*a* (feminine)
Pas un pêcheur dans l'eau,	*b* (masculine)
Pas un falot.	*b* (masculine)
La lune qui s'efface	*c* (feminine)
Couvre son front qui passe	*c* (feminine)
D'un nuage étoilé	*d* (masculine)
Demi-voilé.	*d* (masculine)

In Venice the red,
Not a boat that stirs,
Not a fisherman afloat,
    Not a lantern,

The waning moon
Hides its fading face
With a starlit cloud,
    Half-veiled.

The poem above rhymes in couplets. Where standard quatrains are used, different patterns emerge. For example, Samain's poem "Arpège." set by Fauré, uses rimes croisées:

L'âme d'une flûte soupire	*a* (feminine)
Au fond du parc mélodieux;	*b* (masculine)
Limpide est l'ombre où l'on respire	*a* (feminine)
Ton poème silencieux,	*b* (masculine)

Nuit de langueur, nuit de mensonge,	*c* (feminine)
Qui poses d'un geste ondoyant	*d* (masculine)
Dans ta chevelure de songe	*c* (feminine)
La lune, bijou d'Orient.	*d* (masculine)

The soul of a flute is sighing
Deep in the melodious park;
The shade is limpid where one breathes
Your silent poem,

Night of langour, night of delusion,
That with a flowing gesture
Sets in your dreamy hair
The moon, that Orient jewel.

Within each stanza, therefore, masculine and feminine rhymes alternate.[12]

Why is this focus on rhyme gender and alternation important? First, because the particular sequence of masculine and feminine rhymes in any poem not only helps to determine the sound patterns within the text, but may also allow the poet to create variations in tone (especially if one accepts that rhymes of different gender have intrinsically different qualities). One would not want to push this argument to extremes, but could the contrasting pattern of masculine and feminine rhymes in Ravel's setting of Morand's "Chanson romanesque"[13] not be seen as reinforcing the contrasts in Don Quixote's own address to Dulcinea, which alternates between bluster and solicitude?

Si vous me disiez que la terre	*a* (feminine)
À tant tourner vous offensa,	*b* (masculine)
Je lui dépêcherais Pança:	*b* (masculine)
Vous la verriez fixe et se taire.	*a* (feminine)

Si vous me disiez que l'ennui	*c* (masculine)

Vous vient du ciel trop fleuri d'astres,	*d* (feminine)
Déchirant les divins cadastres,	*d* (feminine)
Je faucherais d'un coup la nuit.	*c* (masculine)

Were you to tell me that the earth
Offended you with so much turning,
I'd despatch Panza to deal with it:
You'd see it still and silenced.

Were you to tell me that you are wearied
By a sky too studded with stars—
Tearing the divine order asunder,
I'd scythe the night with a single blow.

Second, when poets depart from the alternation of masculine and feminine rhymes, we are prompted to ask what effects they are trying to achieve. For instance, does the unbroken sequence of feminine rhymes in Mendès's "Dans la forêt de septembre," set by Fauré, help to subdue the verse and to evoke the forest hush of which the poet speaks?

Ramure aux rumeurs amollies,[14]
Troncs sonores que l'âge creuse,
L'antique forêt douloureuse
S'accorde à nos mélancolies.

Foliage of deadened sound,
Resonant trunks hollowed by age,
The ancient, mournful forest
Blends with our melancholy.

On the other hand, are the insistent masculine rhymes of Verlaine's "En sourdine" a sign that the speaker is much more demanding and impaitient than he would like us to believe?

Calmes dans le demi-jour
Que les branches hautes font
Pénétrons bien notre amour
De ce silence profond.

Calm in the twilight
Cast by the lofty boughs,
Let us steep our love
In this deep quiet.

SOME FINAL THOUGHTS ON RHYME

As one might expect, French verse theorists developed strong views over time about what constituted good practice in rhyming. Some knowledge of their guidelines is valuable, partly to help us understand why certain combinations of rhyme do not appear, partly to help us spot the deliberate transgressions committed by poets such as Verlaine.

By the nineteenth century, for instance, the following practices were considered signs of a poor technique:

- rhyming on words such as "a," "si," or "les"
- rhyming on words with banal associations such as "noir"/"soir"
- rhyming masculine and feminine words such as "folie"/"lit"
- rhyming the same parts of the verb such as "porté"/"donné"
- rhyming singulars with plurals such as "berceau"/"tombeaux"
- rhyming on the same repeated word, though rhyming homonyms, such as "pas" (not) and "pas" (step) is acceptable

The key point is that all these rules were increasingly broken by the poets of the late nineteenth century as part of the freeing-up of verse that I discuss in the next chapter.[15]

SOUND PATTERNING

So far I have concentrated on formal rhyme schemes. But poets use a whole set of other devices to create acoustic patterns in their verse, some involving the rhymes at the end of lines, others linking sounds within the body of the poem. These include the patterning devices described below.

Rhymes that sound much stronger than their formal classification would suggest.[16] In Leconte de Lisle's "Phidylé," set by Duparc, for instance, we find the rhyme "sommeil"/"soleil," which, though technically a rime suffisante, is made much richer by the shared sounds at the beginning of each word.

Alternation of consonant and vowel sounds at the end of lines. In Verlaine's poem "L'ombre des arbres dans la rivière embrumée," all the rhymes are feminine and the formal rhyme scheme is *aabb ccdd*. However, the actual rhyme-sounds create a different pattern: *vvcc ccvv* (where *v* is a vowel sound and *c* a consonant). The acoustic structure of the poem reinforces the patterns of reflection spoken of in the text.

Sequences of rhymes incorporating similar consonants. In Verlaine's poem "Mandoline," for example, the four feminine rhymes in the last verse — extase/grise/jase/brise — all end in "se." This sort of alliteration is known as "contre-assonance" in French.

Internal rhyming. Poets in earlier periods evolved complex patterns that encouraged, for instance, the rhyming of the word at the end of one line with the word at the caesura of the next. By the nineteenth century, verse theorists frowned upon such practices. Nevertheless, in the last verse of Verlaine's poem "Green" we find:

> Toute sonore encor // de vos derniers **baisers**;
> Laissez-la s'ap**aiser** // . . .

> Still ringing with your recent kisses;
> After love's sweet tumult grant it peace

In Baudelaire's "La vie antérieure," set by Duparc, the words at the caesuras of lines 1 and 3 are potential rhymes (habité/piliers), as are the words at the caesuras of lines 5 and 8 (roulant/couchant).

Clustering of similar sounds within the line. In Baudelaire's "La vie antérieure," for instance, we find phrases such as "Les houles, en roulant" and "Aux couleurs du couchant," where vowels and consonants are repeated and reinforce each other within the text.

What is the impact of such sound patterning? Modern commentators are rightly sceptical of claims that particular sounds can evoke specific moods or meanings. On the other hand, poets do clearly use acoustic patterns for expressive effect. So while it might be a little far-fetched to suggest that the repeated "-bre" sounds in the first line of Verlaine's "L'ombre des arbres . . ." conjure up the tangled vegetation of the river bank, there is no doubt that the repetitions give the line a density and complexity that contrast markedly with the much simpler and lighter line that follows, reinforcing the sense of dissipating shadow.[17]

> L'ombre des arbres dans la rivière embrumée
> Meurt comme de la fumée

> The shadow of trees in the misty stream
>   Dies like smoke

Baudelaire's sound clusters in "La vie antérieure," to take another example, help to suggest the blending of sensory perceptions (synesthesia) of which the poem speaks, particularly as phrases such as "rafraîchissaient le front" flow over the traditional metrical juncture at the caesura of the alexandrine.

> Qui me rafraîchissaient // le front avec des palmes

> Who fanned my brows with fronds of palm

Meanwhile, in the final verse of "Mandoline," Verlaine's use of four feminine rhymes ending in a similar consonantal sound, allied to a series of acoustic resonances within the stanza (for instance, with the word "rose") blur the normal distinctions between line endings in a swirling world of sound.

> Tourbillonnent dans l'extase
> D'une lune rose et grise,
> Et la mandoline jase
> Parmi les frissons de brise.

> Whirl madly in the rapture
> Of a grey and roseate moon,
> And the mandolin jangles on
> In the shivering breeze.

7 ✑ Free Verse

THE "VERS LIBRE" OR free verse poems that first
appeared in print in France in 1886, and were subsequently set to
music by composers as different as Chausson, Fauré, and Poulenc, rep-
resented, as we shall see, a fundamental shift in thinking about French
verse. However, many of the innovations of the vers libre can only be
properly understood in the context of developments in verse practice
that had been taking place since well before the end of the nineteenth
century.

This chapter looks briefly at these developments, before examining
the vers libre in more detail. A final section examines different ap-
proaches to reading free verse in French.

EARLY INNOVATIONS

French verse has never been, in reality, as strictly rule-bound as guides
such as this may make it appear. Even during the "classical" period,
between the sixteenth and eighteenth centuries, poets such as La
Fontaine were able to introduce a lot of flexibility into their work (al-
though primarily in light or comic verse), creating what are commonly
referred to as "vers libres classiques" or "vers mêlés." The first six lines
of La Fontaine's fable, "Le corbeau et le renard," set by Caplet, offer an
example.

> Maître corbeau, sur un arbre perché,
> Tenait en son bec un fromage.

Maître renard, par l'odeur alléché,
  Lui tint à peu près ce langage:
  "Et bonjour, Monsieur du Corbeau.
Que vous êtes joli! que vous me semblez beau!"

Master Crow, perched on a tree,
  Was holding in his beak a cheese,
Master Fox, lured by the scent,
  Spoke words more or less like these:
  "Good day, my dear Sir Crow,
How elegant you are! How handsome you look!"

Here La Fontaine mixes lines of 8, 10, and 12 syllables, with the rhyme on "–beau" linking two different meters. The poet is thus able to vary the tempo of the narrative, to create parallelisms within the verse (the two lines beginning "Maître . . ." are both decasyllables) and to exploit the properties of different meters in order to suggest different tones of voice—the gross flattery of the last line is unsurprisingly framed in an alexandrine.

Note, however, that the standard rules on counting syllables and on alternating masculine and feminine rhymes continue to be followed. The decasyllables and the alexandrine also have their caesuras in the regular place.

By the early nineteenth century, however, the shape of the alexandrine was under pressure. Poets such as Hugo, through their use of syntax, began to override the traditional caesura at its center, creating what is often referred to as the "alexandrin trimètre" or "alexandrin romantique."[1] Hugo's "À une femme" (set by Liszt as "Enfant, si j'étais roi") contains the following line, for example:

Si j'étais Dieu, la terr(e) et l'air avec les ondes

If I were God—the earth and the air and the waves

Although the normal caesura at the sixth syllable ("te//rre") is still technically possible, the line divides much more naturally into a 4 + 4 + 4 reading,[2] thus:

> Si j'étais Dieu, / la terre et l'air / avec les ondes

The balance of the traditional line has been upset and the caesura at the sixth syllable, so important in classical alexandrines, is a much attenuated presence. On the other hand, in this poem as in others, Hugo again follows all the standard rules on syllable count and rhyme alternation.

THE VERS LIBÉRÉ

In the second half of the nineteenth century, poets such as Verlaine, Rimbaud, and Mallarmé began to take even greater liberties with what were considered the rules of good verse, creating what is known as the "vers libéré."

We have already seen examples of some of their innovations—poems written entirely in masculine or feminine rhymes, for instance, and the more extensive use of lines with odd-numbered syllables (the vers impair).

Enjambments also became increasingly bold. In Verlaine's "Mandoline," for example, the syntax continues across from the third to the fourth stanzas:

> Leurs courtes vestes de soie,
> Leurs longues robes à queues,
> Leur élégance, leur joie
> Et leurs molles ombres bleues
>
> Tourbillonnent dans l'extase
> D'une lune rose et grise,
>
> . . . .

Their short silken doublets,
Their long trailing gowns,
Their elegance, their joy,
And their soft blue shadows

Whirl madly in the rapture
Of a grey and roseate moon,

. . . .

Meanwhile, the caesura at the sixth syllable of the alexandrine, al-
ready assuming a ghostly form in some of Hugo's lines, was now almost
completely effaced in parts of the vers libéré. How does one segment a
line such as the following, taken from Mallarmé's poem "Soupir," set
by both Debussy and Ravel?

Monte, comme dans un jardin mélancoliqu(e)

Rises…as in some melancholy garden

The line has twelve syllables, but the traditional caesura at the sixth
syllable would fall between "un" and "jardin," which is highly irregular.
We are forced to consider alternatives, such as a 2′ + 6 + 4 reading,
where "monte" is followed by a coupe lyrique.[3] The alexandrine has
become even more destabilized.[4]

What, then, remained of classical precepts? First, syllabic regular-
ity—for all their experiments with the structure of the line, the poets of
the vers libéré continued to count syllables and to follow the rules
of the mute e in largely traditional ways. Second, rhyme—despite a
loosening-up of rhyming practice, and a flouting of the rules discussed
in Chapter 6, poets such as Verlaine and Mallarmé generally perse-
vered in using rhyme to delineate line endings and stanzas.

THE VERS LIBRE

The free verse poems that were published from 1886 onwards made a final assault on these remaining bastions of French verse form.

The vers libre had very diverse origins.[5] Developments in regular verse, the influence of translations (particularly of Whitman) and of popular song, the rediscovery of pre-classical verse freedoms, the language of the Bible, all played their part in its development. Although it brought technical innovation, the vers libre was as much a different way of thinking about verse. As one commentator has suggested, the vers libre "psychologized" French verse.[6] No longer would the poet's imagination and expression be constrained by externally imposed rules on line lengths or rhyme schemes; rather, verse would express the poet's mind, in all its complexity, in language that was both flexible and modern. Traditional meter was dethroned in the search for the poet's personal rhythm; verse form became individualized.

In this quest for psychological authenticity, any element of a poem could be varied. Line lengths might range from the very short to the very long. In Apollinaire's poem "Dans le jardin d'Anna," set by Poulenc, we find the following lines:

> Est-ce bien la date que vous déchiffrez Anna sur
> ce banc de pierre (line 2)
> Du jambon (line 28)

> That is I take it the date you decipher Anna on this
> stone bench
> Ham

The former would be 18 syllables long according to a traditional syllable-count, the latter 3 syllables.

The layout of a poem could also be subject to radical experimentation. Apollinaire's "Bleuet" offers a good example, incorporating multiple margins as well as a line that cuts diagonally across the page.[7]

Meanwhile, poets began to eschew regular rhyming in favor of new mixtures of rhyme, assonance, alliteration, rhymelessness and internal sound-patterning. Éluard's poem "Jacques Villon," also set by Poulenc, is a good example.

1	Irrémédiable vie
2	Vie à toujours chérir
3	En dépit des fléaux
4	Et des morales basses
5	En dépit des étoiles fausses
6	Et des cendres envahissantes
7	En dépit des fièvres grinçantes
8	Des crimes à hauteur du ventre
9	Des seins taris des fronts idiots
10	En dépit des soleils mortels
11	En dépit des dieux morts
12	En dépit des mensonges
13	L'aube l'horizon L'eau
14	L'oiseau l'homme l'amour
15	L'homme léger et bon
16	Adoucissant la terre
17	Éclaircissant les bois
18	Illuminant la pierre
19	Et la rose nocturne
20	Et le sang de la foule.

Irremediable life
Life to be cherished always

Despite scourges
And base morals
Despite false stars
And encroaching ashes

Despite creaking fevers
Belly-high crimes
Dessicated breasts foolish faces
Despite mortal suns

Despite dead gods
Despite the lies
Dawn horizon water
Bird man love

Man light-hearted and good
Sweetening the earth
Clearing the woods
Illuminating the stone

And the nocturnal rose
And the blood of the crowd

Here, the final words of lines 1 and 2 are linked by assonance ("vie"/"chérir"), those ending lines 4 and 5 share common consonants ("basses"/"fausses") while lines 6 and 7 potentially share a full rhyme ("envahissantes"/"grinçantes"), as do lines 16 and 18 ("terre"/"pierre"). Lines 13 and 14, meanwhile, have strong internal sound patterns. However, other parts of the poem, such as the final two lines, neither rhyme nor demonstrate strong sound connections.

Finally, syllable count was challenged, in particular through irregular and ambiguous treatment of the mute e and of contiguous vowels.[8] To give an example, Éluard's "Rayons des yeux et des soleils," once again a Poulenc setting, seems to establish an octosyllabic meter in the first eight lines of the poem, following traditional rules of syllable counting. How then does the reader cope with the two lines that follow, both of which would have 9 syllables according to the normal procedures?

> Je suis un(e) ombre je ne vois plus
> 1 2   3   4   5 6 7   8   9
> Le soleil jaune le soleil roug(e)
> 1 2 3   4   5 6 7 8   9

> I am a shadow I no longer see
> The yellow sun the red sun

One option, encouraged by the parallelisms within the syntax of the two lines, is to suppress the mute e at the end of "ombre" and "jaune,"[9] bringing both lines back to the 8-syllable norm within the poem.[10] However, what authority do we have to apply this procedure in these lines and not elsewhere in the poem? An element of uncertainty has been introduced into the whole reading process.

THE IMPACT OF FREE VERSE

We must be careful not to overstress the impact of free verse. The vers libre did not mean the end of regular verse. Of Chausson's five settings from Maeterlinck's collection *Serres chaudes*, for instance, four of the texts are broadly traditional in construction.[11] Later poets, such as Apollinaire, continued to produce poems with standard syllable counts and rhymes alongside their free verse output.

The advent of free verse did mean, however, that the use of rhyme and traditional meters could henceforth be interpreted as a positive choice by the poet, rather than as something imposed from outside. Poets such as Aragon locate their work within a certain French tradition through their use of regular forms, and the resonances that these forms create can enhance the meaning of particular poems. It is no surprise, for instance, that Aragon's poem "C," so memorably set by Poulenc, is in a traditional 8-syllable meter and, through its single repeated rhyme, makes subtle reference to the sequences of assonances found in medieval French verse.

The vers libre also introduced a new element of unpredictability into French versification. No longer could regularity be taken for granted, and traditional ways of approaching French verse—emphasizing the stresses on the sixth and twelfth syllables of the alexandrine, giving priority to the rhymes at the end of lines over other sorts of acoustic pattern, and so on—were thrown into the melting pot. In many ways, therefore, the vers libre transfers responsibility for finding a way into the verse back onto the individual reader. His or her individual decisions on where to place the stresses in a particular poem, on what sound patterns to emphasize, or on how to handle each mute e in the text, will have a major bearing on how the poem is interpreted.[12]

READING THE VERS LIBRE

What approaches, then, can one take to the vers libre? Clearly, given the emphasis on freedom and personal expression, free verse poems can potentially come in as many different forms as there are poets. However, there are three broad variations worth highlighting.

MIXED REGULAR AND FREE VERSE

In these poems, lines that are broadly regular in shape are mixed with free verse features to create something that is simultaneously traditional and modern. A good example here is Apollinaire's "Sanglots," set by Poulenc, where lines of 12 and 8 syllables, following the normal rules of syllable counting, predominate.[13]

> Et du retour joyeux des heureux émigrants
> 1　2　3　4　　5　6　　7　　8　　9　　10 11 12
> De ce cœur il coulait du sang
> 1　2　　3　　4　　5　6　　7　　8

And the joyous return of happy emigrants
This heart ran with blood

However, these lines are not set out in any regular sequence and other lines are mixed in; the fourth line contains 7 syllables, for instance, and the penultimate line 5 syllables. Also the variations in margin, the lack of punctuation, and the overall lack of rhyme (although combined with strong sound repetition in parts of the poem—"conquérants"/"émigrants"/"sang"/"pensant") make this visibly a free verse poem.

ACCENTED VERSE

In these poems, there is no regular syllable count, but the syntax and punctuation continue to focus our attention on individual lines and, in particular, on repeated patterns of accentuation. In Rimbaud's "Marine,"[14] for instance, the syllable count for the lines varies between 4 and 13. On the other hand, most of the lines seem to divide naturally into two accented phrases, encouraging us to find a regular rhythm in our reading.

> Les chars d'argent / et de cuivre—
> Les proues d'acier / et d'argent—
> Bat / tent l'écume,—
> Soulèvent les souches / des ronces,
>
> . . . .
>
> Chariots of silver and copper—
> Prows of steel and silver—
> Thrash the foam—
> Rip up the bramble roots,
>
> . . . .

VERSE BASED ON SMALL RHYTHMIC SECTIONS

In these poems, a reading based on small-scale rhythmic pulses is preferable, typically (but not exclusively) because the verse contains lines that have become almost too long for the reader to encompass.[15] For example, in Robert Desnos's poem "Les espaces du sommeil," set by Lutoslawski, the first line would have almost 30 syllables according to traditional rules of syllable counting. It makes sense therefore to approach the text in terms of a series of subsections, which together make up the line.

> Dans la nuit / il y a naturellement / les sept
> merveilles du monde / et la grandeur / et le
> tragique / et le charme.

> In the night there are of course the seven wonders
> of the world and greatness and tragedy and
> mystery.

Note that these phrases are no longer conventional subdivisions of a pre-existing line, as they would be in regular verse; rather, the repeated pulses themselves are the motivating force behind the verse and it is their combination that creates the shape of each individual line.

FREE VERSE: SOME FINAL THOUGHTS

Two final points are worth making.

First, all these different ways of approaching free verse (and, indeed, other approaches) are available to the reader simultaneously and may be applied in the same poem. It is for the reader to decide what is most helpful.

Second, as will have become apparent, even in the vers libre, French verse remains resolutely French and can only be fully understood in the context of its own history, traditions, and concerns.

Commentaries on
Four Poems

"*ADIEUX DE L'HÔTESSE ARABE*" *BY VICTOR HUGO* (*1802–1885*)

1	Puisque rien / ne t'arrête // en cet heureux / pays,	3 + 3 + 4 + 2
2	Ni l'om/bre du palmier, // ni le jeu/ne maïs,	2 + 4 + 3 + 3
3	Ni le repos, / ni l'abondance,	4 + 4
4	Ni de voir / à ta voix // ba/ttre le jeune sein	3 + 3 + 1 + 5
5	De nos sœurs, / dont, les soirs, // le tournoyant / essaim	3 + 3 + 4 + 2
6	Couro/nne un coteau / de sa danse,	2 + 3 + 3
7	Adieu, beau voyageur! Hélas adieu! Oh! que n'es-tu de ceux	(modified line)[1]
8	Qui do/nnent pour limite // à leurs pieds / paresseux	2 + 4 + 3 + 3
9	Leur toit / de bran/ches ou de toiles!	2 + 2 + 4
10	Qui, rêveurs, / sans en faire, // écou/tent les récits,	3 + 3 + 2 + 4
11	Et souhai/tent, le soir, // devant leur po/rte assis,	3 + 3 + 4 + 2
12	De s'en aller / dans les étoiles!	4 + 4

13	Si tu l'avais / voulu, // peut-ê/tre une de nous,	4 + 2 + 2 + 4
14	Ô jeune ho/mme, eût aimé // te servir // à genoux	3 + 3 + 3 + 3
15	Dans nos hu/ttes toujours ouvertes;	3 + 5
16	Elle eût fait, / en berçant // ton sommeil // de tes chants,	3 + 3 + 3 + 3
17	Pour chasser / de ton front // les moucherons / méchants,	3 + 3 + 4 + 2
18	Un éventail / de feui/lles vertes.	4 + 2 + 2
19	Si tu ne reviens pas, // songe un peu / quelquefois	6 + 3 + 3
20	Aux fi/lles du désert, // sœurs / à la douce voix,	2 + 4 + 1 + 5
21	Qui dan/sent pieds nus / sur la dune;	2 + 3 + 3
22	Ô beau jeune ho/mme blanc, // bel oiseau / passager,	4 + 2 + 3 + 3
23	Souviens-toi, / car peut-être, // ô rapi/de étranger,	3 + 3 + 3 + 3
24	Ton souvenir / re/ste à plus d'une!	4 + 1 + 3
25	Hélas! Adieu! bel étranger! Souviens-toi!	(inserted line)

Since nothing can keep you in this happy land,
Neither shade-giving palm nor yellow corn,
    Nor repose nor abundance,
Nor the sight of our sisters' young breasts trembling
At your voice as, in wheeling throng at evening,
    They garland a hillside with their dance,

Farewell, fair traveller! Ah! Why are you not like
    those
Whose indolent feet venture no further
    Than their roofs of branch or canvas!

Who, musing, listen passively to tales
And dream at evening, sitting before their door,
   Of wandering among the stars!

Had you so wished, perhaps one of us,
O young man, would willingly have served you,
    kneeling,
   In our ever-open huts;
Lulling you asleep with songs, she would have made,
To chase the tiresome midges from your brow,
   A fan of green leaves.

If you do not return, dream at times
Of the daughters of the desert, sweet-voiced sisters,
   Who dance barefoot on the dunes;
O handsome young white man, fair bird of passage,
Remember—for perhaps, O fleeting stranger,
   More than one maiden will remember you!

Alas! Farewell, fair stranger! Remember!

Hugo wrote "Adieux de l'hôtesse arabe" in 1828 and the poem was published the following year in the collection *Les Orientales*. Bizet composed his setting during 1866, using four of Hugo's original eight stanzas. One line is heavily modified and one added (lines 7 and 25 above). Graham Johnson has described the song as a "haunting masterpiece" and "perhaps the greatest of all the oriental evocations in French music" for piano and voice.[2]

Hugo's orientalism was not, however, his most significant contribution to the history of nineteenth-century French literature—other authors such as Chateaubriand (as well as painters like Delacroix and Boulanger) had similar interests in the exotic. Rather, it is the poet's extraordinary range of expression and what one critic has called his "unsurpassed ability to invent new metrical forms adapted to whatever scene he is describing"[3] that most distinguish Hugo's early collections of verse.

In "Adieux de l'hôtesse arabe," Hugo mixes 12-syllable with 8-syllable lines. The poem therefore combines the traditional weightiness of the alexandrine—the young woman is, after all, losing not just a lover but almost certainly a source of economic support—with the rhythmic flexibility of the octosyllabic, a meter often associated with song. Note how the poet arranges the rhyme scheme *aabccb* to ensure that all the alexandrines end in masculine rhymes (the young man is, of course, a soldier, as the full text of Hugo's poem makes clear) and all the octosyllables in feminine rhymes. It is almost as if the dialogue between the young people were being mirrored in the very structure of the verse.

Within the individual lines, Hugo exploits the potential for variation to the full. As the scansion above suggests, the fifteen alexandrines display nine different rhythmic combinations (3 + 3 + 4 + 2 and so on). The octosyllables are even more diverse—six distinct rhythms within the eight lines in my analysis. Equally striking is the way in which the poet makes extensive use of the coupe enjambante, where the mute e ending a word is carried forward into the syllable count for the following word group. Line 2 alone offers two examples on "om/bre" and "jeu/ne." The verse therefore has an ever-shifting and undulating quality that prefigures Bizet's musical setting.

The structure of the regular alexandrine focuses the reader's attention on the sixth and twelfth syllables—that is, on the end of the line and on the mid-line caesura. In the first stanza, the words placed at these positions ("arrête," "pays," "palmier," "maïs," "voix," "sein," "soirs," "essaim") already contain the essence of the young woman's plea. "Stay with us in this exotic land," she seems to say, "and take advantage of the swarm of sexual possibilities". Note also how the enjambments at the ends of lines 4 and 5 contribute to a sense of a swirling dance, while at the same time emphasizing the phrases "De nos sœurs" and "couronne." Ruling over a harem may be many a soldier's fantasy and the hôtesse plays up the possibility to the limit.

The second and third stanzas continue the exploration of what is on offer to the young man. Does one get a hint, in the disrupted syntax of lines 10 and 11, that the reveries of which the woman speaks may be drug-induced, almost as if fragments of the tales were coming and going in the listener's consciousness?[4] The rhythm of lines 16 and 17, allied to the internal rhyme "berçant"/"chants" and the repetition of the sound "ch," certainly serve to evoke a gentle song, the segmentation of the two lines into 3-syllable groups only interrupted by the 4 + 2 hemistich that introduces "les moucherons méchants."

The last stanza looks to a future where the young woman and her colleagues will be thrown back on their own sisterhood (note the prominence given to the word "sœurs" by the rhythm of line 20). Bizet's setting ends perhaps on a more enigmatic note than Hugo's original poem, which continues for another stanza. Just what romantic attachments or unfulfilled desires is the young man leaving behind? The placing of "peut-être" at the caesura of the final alexandrine may suggest that the hôtesse knows more than she is letting on.

Two final points should be made. First, the use of 6-line stanzas (or sizains) in preference to the more common and pithier quatrain or 4-line stanza allows the poem to unroll in a long-breathed and languorous way. Second, virtually all the rhymes in Bizet's four stanzas are "riches," as they are throughout Hugo's original poem, infusing a lushness into the verse that complements all the other techniques the poet has used to evoke the wonders of the Orient.

"LE COLIBRI" BY CHARLES LECONTE DE LISLE (1818–1894)

1   Le vert colibri, le roi des collines,

2   Voyant la rosée et le soleil clair

3   Luire dans son nid tissé d'herbes fines,

4   Comme un frais rayon s'échappe dans l'air.

5   Il se hâte et vole aux sources voisines

6   Où les bambous font le bruit de la mer,

7   Où l'açoka rouge, aux odeurs divines,
8   S'ouvre et porte au cœur un humide éclair.

9   Vers la fleur dorée il descend, se pose,
10   Et boit tant d'amour dans la coupe rose,
11   Qu'il meurt, ne sachant s'il l'a pu tarir.

12   Sur ta lèvre pure, ô ma bien-aimée,
13   Telle aussi mon âme eût voulu mourir
14   Du premier baiser qui l'a parfumée!

The green humming-bird, the king of the hills,
On seeing the dew and gleaming sun
Shine in his nest of fine woven grass,
Darts into the air like a shaft of light.

He hurries and flies to the nearby springs
Where the bamboos sound like the sea,
Where the red hibiscus with its heavenly scent
Unveils the glint of dew at its heart.

He descends, and settles on the golden flower,
Drinks so much love from the rosy cup
That he dies, not knowing if he'd drunk it dry.

On your pure lips, O my beloved,
My own soul too would sooner have died
From that first kiss which scented it!

"Le colibri" was first published in 1855 in Leconte de Lisle's collection *Poëmes et Poésies*. The poem later became part of the collection *Poèmes barbares*. It has been set by a number of composers, most notably Chausson.

"Le colibri" is a sonnet whose tercets follow the regular *ccd ede* rhyme scheme. The two quatrains, however, are in rimes croisées (*abab*) rather than in the more traditional rimes embrassées (*abba*), giving the bird's search for the ultimately fatal flower a strong forward momentum and urgency. Note, also, that the volta in this sonnet, where the poet gives meaning to the poem's central image, only comes after the eleventh line, prolonging the bird's life and perhaps also the memory of that first kiss which is the inspiration for the poet.

The poem is in a 10-syllable or decasyllabic meter. The opening line establishes a 5 + 5 division of the syllables, with a central caesura—a pattern that frequently replaced the more traditional 4 + 6 structure in nineteenth century lyric poetry.

> Le vert colibri // le roi des collin(es),
> 1 2 3 4 5 6 7 8 9 10

This pattern continues throughout the poem until line 11, where the meaning, punctuation, and syntax encourage us to shift our focus from the central caesura towards the break after the second syllable.

> Qu'il meurt, / ne sachant // s'il l'a pu tarir.
> 1   2   3 4 5   6 7 8 9 10

Coming immediately after lines 9 and 10, where the couplet, with its rhymes "pose"/"rose," has given a particular solidity to the verse, this rhythmic displacement, and therefore the bird's death, is doubly shocking. However, this is a poem about life rather than death and the 5 + 5 balance of the line is immediately restored in line 12.

> Sur ta lèvre pur(e), // ô ma bien-aimé(e),

Two further points are worth making about the verse structure. First, the 5 + 5 division of the decasyllable, as we noted in Chapter 3, brings an uncertainty about how many stresses to give each line. The temptation must be to give line 5 only three stresses, for example, to suggest the movement of the bird.

> Il se hât(e) et **vol**(e) // aux **sou**/rces voisin(es)
> (5 + 2 + 3)

In contrast, line 8 would seem to warrant four stresses in order to emphasize the opening of the flower and its magical effect.

> **S'ou**/vr(e) et port(e) au **coeur** // un humi/d(e) éclair
> (1 + 4 + 3 +2)

Such rhythmic options and ambiguities pervade the poem, mirroring perhaps the gyrations of both the hummingbird and the poet's own feelings.

Second, within a regular rhyme scheme, with the traditional alternation of masculine and feminine rhymes, the poet has managed to put rhyme degree to both structural and expressive use.

Of the first five rhymes in the poem, four are merely suffisantes (the exception is the rime riche of "clair"/"l'air"). However, as the intensity of the poem increases and as the poet arrives at his declaration of love, the rhymes become stronger; the last two rhyme pairs ("tarir"/"mourir" and "bien-aimée"/"parfumée") are both rimes riches according to the traditional classification.

The rhyme "tarir"/"mourir" therefore provides a robust bridge between the body of the poem and the final tercet, while at the same time underlining the sonnet's central conceit: "Drink deep of love and suffer a (poetic) death." On the other hand, the concentration of stronger rhymes at the very end of the poem only serves to highlight the fact that, for all its exoticism, the image of the hummingbird is merely a vehicle for exploring what is truly important to the narrator — his love-struck heart.

"EN SOURDINE" BY PAUL VERLAINE (1844–1896)

1	Calmes / dans le demi-jour	2′ + 5
2	Que les bran/ches hau/tes font	3 + 2 + 2
3	Pénétrons bien / notre amour	4 + 3
4	De ce silen/ce profond.	4 + 3
5	Fondons⁵ nos â/mes, nos coeurs	4 + 3
6	Et nos sens / extasiés,	3 + 4
7	Parmi les va/gues langueurs	4 + 3
8	Des pins / et des arbusiers.	2 + 5
9	Ferme tes yeux / à demi,	4 + 3
10	Croise tes bras / sur ton sein,	4 + 3
11	Et de ton coeur / endormi	4 + 3
12	Chasse à jamais / tout dessein.	4 + 3
13	Laissons-nous / persuader	3 + 4
14	Au souffle berceur / et doux,	5 + 2
15	Qui vient / à tes pieds / rider	2 + 3 + 2 (5 + 2)
16	Les on/des de gazon roux.	2 + 5
17	Et quand, / solennel, / le soir	2 + 3 + 2
18	Des chênes noirs / tombera,	4 + 3
19	Voix / de notre désespoir,	1 + 6
20	Le rossignol / chantera.	4 + 3

Calm in the twilight
Cast by lofty boughs,
Let us steep our love
In this deep quiet.

Let us mingle our souls, our hearts
And our enraptured senses

With the hazy languor
Of arbutus and pine.

Half-close your eyes,
Fold your arms across your breast,
And from your heart now lulled to rest
Banish forever all intent.

Let us both succumb
To the gentle and lulling breeze
That comes to ruffle at your feet
The waves of russet grass.

And when, solemnly, evening
Falls from the black oaks,
That voice of our despair
The nightingale shall sing.

This poem was first published in the magazine *L'Artiste* in July 1868 and was subsequently included in the first full edition of Verlaine's *Fêtes galantes*, which appeared the following year. It has been set many times, most notably by Debussy, Fauré, and Hahn.

The poem is in a 7-syllable meter, a vers impair which has links with song (and therefore directs our attention to the importance of the nightingale's intervention at the end of the poem) but which was also used deliberately by poets such as Verlaine to suggest unbalanced, even anxious states. The meter sits between dual-accented hexasyllable (6-syllable line) and the decasyllable or 10-syllable line, which has three main stresses in its traditional 4 + 6 form. Although many of the lines in the poem fall happily into a two-accent pattern, some (such as lines 2 and 17) seem to invite a three-accent reading, while others (such as line 15) are ambiguous, giving an overall instability to the versification.

We are in a world of Verlainian erotic discontent, therefore, and the poetic voice may be much less confident than it first seems.

A number of features in the verse lend weight to this suspicion. The rhymes are all masculine, for instance, breaking with the tradition of alternating rhyme genders. This is not a two-way conversation, but one where an insistent, even wheedling, male voice tries to impose its own vision of erotic satisfaction on a partner, whose response, were she (or he) given the chance to answer, might not be positive.

The stanzaic structure reinforces this interpretation. Where one might expect to find the more inward-looking rimes embrassées (*abba*), instead the five stanzas are all in rimes croisées (*abab*), as if the speaker has constantly to invent new arguments to support his position.

My detailed scansion of the poem, set out above, suggests that the rhythm of the verse develops in three distinct phases. In the first two stanzas, the speaker appears to be making almost a conscious effort to mute the emotional temperature, and the rhythm edges towards a balanced 4 + 3 division of the line. We might imagine the word "calmes" as an invocation and apply a coupe lyrique, giving a 2′ + 5 reading of the first line. Interestingly, lines 2 and 8, where nature is invoked, are both out of kilter with the prevailing rhythm in this part of the poem, suggesting that the surroundings are less serene than the speaker might like to admit.

In the third stanza, the narrator seems to have achieved his aim, with the 4 + 3 rhythm in control, lulling the poet's partner (and us) to sleep. It is almost certainly no coincidence that the rhymes here are consistently riches, whereas in the first two stanzas they have varied in degree.

The rhythmic calm of the third stanza does not hold, however, and the last two stanzas display, if anything, an even greater range of rhythmic variation than we encountered at the beginning of the poem. The rhythmic disruption in this part of the poem is increased by the rather cacophonous juxtaposition of "pieds" and "rider" in line 15, the enjambment at the end of line 17 and the heavy stress on "voix" that unbalances line 19. The rhymes too become unsettled with a rime pauvre (doux/roux) appearing for the first time, while the force of the final rhyme (tombera/chantera)—technically léonine—is much reduced by the rhyme being based on the same part of the verb. The effect is almost that of parody.

All the signs in the verse are, then, that the nightingale's song, when it finally appears in a line whose 4 + 3 rhythm serves as a mocking reminder of the tranquillity sought and lost in the third stanza, is truly a voice of despair.

"MONTPARNASSE" BY GUILLAUME APOLLINAIRE (1880–1918)

1	Ô porte de l'hôtel avec deux plantes vertes
2	Vertes qui jamais
3	Ne porteront de fleurs
4	Où sont mes fruits Où me planté-je
5	Ô porte de l'hôtel un ange est devant toi
6	Distribuant des prospectus
7	On n'a jamais si bien défendu la vertu
8	Donnez-moi pour toujours une chambre à la semaine
9	Ange barbu vous êtes en réalité
10	Un poète lyrique d'Allemagne
11	Qui voulez connaître Paris
12	Vous connaissez de son pavé
13	Ces raies sur lesquelles il ne faut pas que l'on marche
14	Et vous rêvez
15	D'aller passer votre Dimanche à Garches
16	Il fait un peu lourd et vous cheveux sont longs
17	Ô bon petit poète un peu bête et trop blond
18	Vos yeux ressemblent tant à ces deux gros ballons
19	Qui s'ont vont dans l'air pur
20	À l'aventure

O hotel door with two green plants
Green which shall never
Bear any flowers
Where are my fruits Where did I plant myself

O hotel door an angel stands before you
Distributing prospectuses
Virtue has never been so well defended
Give me for ever a room by the week
Bearded angel you are in reality
A lyric poet from Germany
Who wants to know Paris
You know its pavements'
Lines where you must not step
  And you dream
Of spending your Sunday at Garches

It's somewhat oppressive and your hair is long
O good little poet rather stupid and too blonde
Your eyes so resemble those two big balloons
Which float away in the pure air
Haphazardly

Apollinaire wrote "Montparnasse" in 1912. It first appeared in the magazine *Vers et prose* in late 1913 and was later included in the collection *Il y a*, which was published in 1925, seven years after the poet's death. Poulenc worked on fragments of the poem over several years before the whole song came together in three days in February 1945.

The narrator (perhaps the poet himself as an older man) transports us to a magical time when a young poet discovers Paris. We sense that this discovery will not only confirm the young man in his artistic vocation (despite the miseries of daily life) but will also furnish him with the very material of his poetry—life in the city.

The poem is suffused with the religious, mythical, and poetic allusions that abound in Apollinaire's work. The young poet is almost Christ-like in both his purity and his appearance. The very name Montparnasse evokes Mount Parnassus, the sacred home of Apollo and the Muses, which gave its name to the important nineteenth century Parnassian school of French poetry.

At the same time, "Montparnasse" is very definitely a work of the twentieth century—a poem of discontinuous form, sudden shifts of narrative perspective, "unpoetic" words and no punctuation, a poem capable of celebrating fake plants, seedy hotels, and the cracks in pavements.

It is no surprise, then, that the verse itself sits in a no-man's-land between the traditional and the modern. Applying the normal rules of syllable counting, for instance, we discover that lines of 6, 8, 10, and 12 syllables predominate. The very first line could easily be read as a regular alexandrine with a caesura at the sixth syllable, as could lines 5, 17, and 18.

> Ô port/e de l'hôtel // avec deux plan/tes vert(es)
> (2 + 4 + 4 + 2)

Line 7 has more of the tripartite structure of the alexandrin romantique, but would not have been out of place in the work of poets such as Verlaine.

On the other hand, a number of lines do not fit neatly into traditional categories. Lines 8 and 13 have 13 and 14 syllables, respectively, according to a normal syllable count. Do we leave them as they are or try to bring them back to a 12-syllable norm by suppressing the mute e on "un(e)," "rai(es)," and "lesquell(es)"? Line 16, meanwhile, with its 11 syllables, has no mute e to play with, so do we accept it as it is, or interpret it as an alexandrine that is slightly down at heel (like the young poet himself) or as a decasyllable that has aspirations beyond its station?

The very fact that these options exist in some lines throws the status of all the lines into question, particularly as there is no regular pattern in the sequence of different meters deployed in the poem. Why should we not suppress the mute e on "port(e)" or "plant(es)" in the first line, for instance, if we are doing so elsewhere, thereby creating a decasyllable with strong demotic overtones. The reader has to make his or her own choices on how to read the poem in a way that is not required in traditional verse.

The poem has no regular rhyme scheme, and masculine and feminine and singular and plural line endings are mixed. However, there are occasions where repeated patterns of sounds seem to be used deliberately to bind together subsections of the poem. The parallel sequences "connaissez"/"pavé"/"marche" and "rêvez"/"aller"/"passer" /"Garches" in lines 12 to 15 are an example.

As the poem reaches its climax, the emotional temperature is raised by the sudden concentration of rhymes at the end of lines 16 to 18 ("longs"/"blond"/"ballons," with an internal rhyme on "vont") and 19 to 20 ("pur"/"aventure"), almost as if a moment of supreme poetic inspiration has been reached. Note also the transition from the abrupt masculine rhymes of "longs"/"blond"/"ballons" through the masculine rhyme "pur" with its sounded consonant to its open-ended feminine rhyme-partner "aventure," where the mute e extends the preceding syllable and helps to suggest how the balloons (and, by implication, the poet's spirit) rise unfettered in the ether.

Poem	Poet	Collection	Major settings
1904	Apollinaire	*Il y a*	Poulenc
À Cassandre	Ronsard	*Le second livre des odes*	Leguerney (as "À sa maîtresse")
À Clymène	Verlaine	*Fêtes galantes*	Fauré
Adieux de l'hôtesse arabe	Hugo	*Les orientales*	Bizet
Arpège	Samain	*Au jardin de l'infante*	Fauré
Attente	Hugo	*Les orientales*	Saint-Saëns (as "L'attente")
Au bord de l'eau	Sully Prudhomme	*Les vaines tendresses*	Fauré
Au cimetière	Richepin	*La mer*	Fauré
À une femme	Hugo	*Les feuilles d'automne*	Liszt (as "Enfant, si j'étais roi")
Ballade des femmes de Paris	Villon	*Le testament*	Debussy
Ballade des gros dindons	Rostand	None	Chabrier
Ballade pour prier Nostre Dame	Villon	*Le testament*	Debussy (as "Ballade que Villon feit à la requeste de sa mère pour prier Nostre-Dame")
Bleuet	Apollinaire	*Il y a*	Poulenc
C	Aragon	*Les yeux d'Elsa*	Poulenc
Chanson	Régnier	*La sandale ailée*	Fauré
Chanson XIII	Marot	*L'adolescence clémentine*	Enescu (as "Languir me fais")
Chanson d'automne	Verlaine	*Poèmes saturniens*	Hahn
Chanson romanesque	Morand	Not found*	Ravel
Chanson triste	Lahor	*L'illusion* (in section *Chants de l'amour et de la mort*)	Duparc
Chevaux de bois	Verlaine	*Romances sans paroles*	Debussy
Clair de lune	Verlaine	*Fêtes galantes*	Debussy; Fauré

Colloque sentimental	Verlaine	Fêtes galantes	Debussy
Dans la forêt de septembre	Mendès	Not found*	Fauré
Dans le jardin d'Anna	Apollinaire	Il y a	Poulenc
Dans les ruins d'une abbaye	Hugo	Les chansons des rues et des bois	Fauré
Diane, Séléné	La Ville de Mirmont	L'horizon chimérique	Fauré
Donc, ce sera . . .	Verlaine	La bonne chanson	Fauré
En sourdine	Verlaine	Fêtes galantes	Debussy; Fauré; Hahn
Green	Verlaine	Romances sans paroles	Debussy; Fauré; Hahn (as "Offrande")
Il pleure dans mon cœur	Verlaine	Romances sans paroles	Debussy
Infidélité	Gautier	Poésies	Hahn
Jacques Villon	Éluard	Voir	Poulenc
J'allais par des chemins perfides	Verlaine	La bonne chanson	Fauré
L'absent	Gounod	None	Gounod
La captive	Hugo	Les orientales	Berlioz
La caravane	Gautier	Poésies diverses (published with La comédie de la mort)	Chausson
La dernière pensée de Weber	Banville	Les stalactites	Debussy (as "Nuit d'étoiles")
La dure épreuve va finir	Verlaine	La bonne chanson	Hahn (as "La bonne chanson")
La lune blanche	Verlaine	La bonne chanson	Fauré; Hahn (as "L'heure exquise")
Lamento (Connaissez-vous la blanche tombe)	Gautier	Poésies diverses (published with La comédie de la mort)	Duparc
Lamento (Ma belle amie est morte)	Gautier	Poésies diverses (published with La comédie de la mort)	Berlioz (as "Sur les lagunes"); Fauré (as "La chanson du pêcheur")
La mer est infinie	La Ville de Mirmont	L'horizon chimérique	Fauré
La rose	Leconte de Lisle	Odes anacréontiques (in Poèmes antiques)	Fauré
La vie antérieure	Baudelaire	Les fleurs du mal	Duparc

(continued)

97

Poem	Poet	Collection	Major settings
Le château du Bartas	Bédat de Monlaur	Villanelles	Honegger
Le ciel est, par-dessus le toit	Verlaine	Sagesse	Fauré (as "Prison"); Hahn (as "D'une prison")
Le colibri	Leconte de Lisle	Poèmes barbares	Chausson
Le corbeau et le renard	La Fontaine	Fables	Caplet
L'écrevisse	Apollinaire	Le bestiaire	Poulenc
Le don silencieux	Dominique	L'anémone des mers	Fauré
Le jet d'eau	Baudelaire	Nouvelles fleurs du mal	Debussy
Le long du quai	Sully Prudhomme	Stances et poèmes	Fauré (as "Les berceaux")
Le manoir de Rosemonde	Bonnières	Contes de fées	Duparc
L'enamourée	Banville	Les exilés	Hahn
Le papillon et la fleur	Hugo	Les chants du crépuscule	Fauré
Le parfum impérissable	Leconte de Lisle	Poèmes tragiques	Fauré
Le pas d'armes du roi Jean	Hugo	Odes et ballades	Chabrier; Saint-Saëns
Le printemps	Banville	Les cariatides	Hahn
Le promenoir des deux amants	Tristan l'Hermite	Plaintes d'Acante	Debussy
Les espaces du sommeil	Desnos	Corps et biens	Lutoslawski
Les étoiles	Banville	Poésies	Hahn
Les hiboux	Baudelaire	Les fleurs du mal	Séverac
Le soir	Lamartine	Méditations poétiques	Gounod
Le son du cor s'afflige	Verlaine	Sagesse	Debussy
Les roses d'Ispahan	Leconte de Lisle	Poèmes tragiques	Fauré
Le thé	Banville	Les cariatides	Koechlin
Le vallon	Lamartine	Méditations poétiques	Gounod

L'invitation au voyage	Baudelaire	Les fleurs du mal	Duparc; Chabrier
L'ombre des arbres dans la rivière embrunée	Verlaine	Romances sans paroles	Debussy; Hahn (as "Paysage triste")
Mai	Hugo	Les chants du crépuscule	Fauré
Mandoline	Verlaine	Fêtes galantes	Debussy; Fauré; Hahn (as "Fêtes galantes")
Marine	Rimbaud	Illuminations	Britten
Mes vers fuiraient doux et frêles	Hugo	Les contemplations	Hahn
Nanny	Leconte de Lisle	Chansons écossaises (in Poèmes antiques)	Chausson
N'est-ce pas?	Verlaine	La bonne chanson	Fauré
Nocturne	Cros	Le coffret de santal	Chausson (as "Chanson perpétuelle")
Ode du premier jour de mai	Passerat	None	Gounod (as "Le premier jour de mai")
Oh! quand je dors	Hugo	Les rayons et les ombres	Liszt
O ma belle rebelle	Baïf	Amours de Francine	Gounod
Phidylé	Leconte de Lisle	Poèmes antiques	Duparc
Pierrot	Banville	Les cariatides	Debussy
Pour ce que Plaisance est morte	Charles d'Orléans	Rondeaux	Debussy
Quand je fus pris au pavillon	Charles d'Orléans	Rondeaux	Hahn
Quand la nuit n'est pas étoilée	Hugo	Part of poem "Puisque nos heures sont remplies" in Les chants du crépuscule	Hahn
Quand tu plonges tes yeux dans mes yeux	Van Lerberghe	Entrevisions	Fauré (in Le jardin clos)
Rayons des yeux et des soleils	Éluard	Le livre ouvert I (part of poem "Vue donne vie")	Poulenc

(continued)

99

APPENDIX TWO *Poems and Songs Discussed in the Guide* (continued)

Poem	Poet	Collection	Major settings
Recueillement	Baudelaire	*Nouvelles fleurs du mal*	Debussy
Rencontre	Grandmougin	Not found*	Fauré
Romance (Au pays où se fait la guerre)	Gautier	*Poésies diverses* (published with *La comédie de la mort*)	Duparc
Sanglots	Apollinaire	*Il y a*	Poulenc
Sonnet (Mon âme a son secret)	Arvers	*Mes heures perdues*	Bizet (as "Ma vie a son secret")
Soupir	Mallarmé	*Poésies*	Debussy; Ravel
Soupir	Sully Prudhomme	*Les solitudes*	Duparc
Spleen	Verlaine	*Romances sans paroles*	Debussy
Surgi de la croupe et du bond	Mallarmé	*Poésies*	Ravel
Vaisseaux . . .	La Ville de Mirmont	*L'horizon chimérique*	Fauré
Venise	Musset	*Premières poésies*	Gounod
Villanelle des petits canards	Gérard	*Les pipeaux*	Chabrier

*It has proved difficult to trace the collections in which some of the less well-known poems originally appeared. I would be interested to hear from anyone who knows the original sources.

A Brief History of
French Versification

Date	Poets in the Guide	Key developments in versification
900		Origins of 8-syllable line (octosyllable)
1000		Origins of 10-syllable line (decasyllable)
1100		Origins of 12-syllable line
1200		
1300		Ballade form appears in French verse
		Origins of the rondel
1400	Charles d'Orléans (1391–1465)	12-syllable line becomes known as "alexandrin"
	Villon (1431–after 1463)	
1500	Marot (1496–1544)	Sonnet and villanelle forms appear in French verse
	Ronsard (1524–85)	
	Baïf (1532–89)	
	Passerat (1534–1602)	To alternate rhyme genders becomes accepted practice
1600		Alexandrine eclipses decasyllable in serious verse
	Tristan l'Hermite (1602–55)	Decasyllable and octosyllable used mainly in light verse
	La Fontaine (1621–95)	Mixing of meters in vers libres classiques
1700		Alexandrine remains main meter for serious verse
		Decasyllable and octosyllable re-establish themselves in lyric verse
1800	Lamartine (1790–1869)	
	Hugo (1802–85)	Alexandrin trimètre exploited by Hugo and others

(continued)

APPENDIX THREE *A Brief History of French Versification* (continued)

Date	Poets in the Guide	Key developments in versification
1850	Arvers (1806–50) Musset (1810–57) Gautier (1811–72) Leconte de Lisle (1818–94)	The sonnet and rondel become increasingly popular
1875	Baudelaire (1821–67) Banville (1823–91) Sully Prudhomme (1839–1907) Lahor (1840–1909) Mallarmé (1842–98) Verlaine (1844–96)	Development of vers libéré Vers impair is used to create more fluid form of verse
1900	Rimbaud (1854–91) Cros (1842–88) Mendès (1842–1909) Richepin (1849–1926) Bonnières (1850–1905) Grandmougin (1850–1930) Samain (1858–1900) Régnier (1864–1936) Van Lerberghe (1861–1907) Rostand (1868–1918) Gérard (1866–1953) Dominique (1875–1952) Apollinaire (1880–1918) La Ville de Mirmont (1886–1914)	First free verse poems published (1886) Poets increasingly break traditional rules governing: • Syllable counting and treatment of mute e
1925–	Morand (1888–1976) Éluard (1895–1952) Aragon (1897–1982) Desnos (1900–45) Bédat de Monlaur (1907–1990)	• Rhyming • Stanzaic forms • Page layout and punctuation

Glossary of Technical Terms

Accent: another word for stress. In French, accent is related to the position of a word in a phrase, rather than to an underlying "beat" as in English.

Accent d'insistance: an accent applied to the opening syllables of a word or word group. Such accents are generally considered to be a personal choice of the reader, rather than something inherent in the verse. Also referred to as "accents oratoires."

Accent oratoire: see *accent d'insistance*.

Alexandrin romantique: see *alexandrin trimètre*.

Alexandrin tétramètre: see *alexandrine*.

Alexandrin trimètre: an *alexandrine* where the meaning and syntax encourage a 3-*measure scansion* rather than the traditional 4-*measure* one. Also sometimes called the "alexandrin romantique."

Alexandrine: a 12-syllable line, traditionally divided into two equal 6-syllable *hemistiches* by a *caesura*. The regular alexandrine is often known as the alexandrin tétramètre because it normally contains four *measures*.

Assonance: the repetition of identical accented vowel sounds in words with dissimilar consonants, e.g. "jade"/"opale."

Ballade: one of the standard fixed forms in French verse. See Chapter 5 for variations, including the ballade primitive, the petite ballade, and the grande ballade.

Caesura: the principal metrical juncture in the line of a *vers composé*. Known as the "césure" in French. The caesura is indicated in *scansion* by two oblique lines //. See also *césure enjambante*, *césure épique*, and *césure lyrique*.

Césure: see caesura.

Césure enjambante: the occurrence of an unelided *mute e* immediately after the *caesura*, e.g. on the seventh syllable of an *alexandrine*. See also *elision*. This type of caesura (as well as the *césure épique* and *césure lyrique*) was proscribed by verse theorists for much of the period between

103

the sixteenth and late nineteenth centuries, but reappears in modern verse.

Césure épique: the occurrence of an uncounted *mute e* that cannot be elided, and would therefore normally be taken into account in determining the number of syllables in a line, immediately before the *caesura*. The césure épique is found in early French literature and reappears in modern verse. See also *elision* and the comments under *césure enjambante* about verse theorists.

Césure lyrique: the placement of an unelided *mute e* immediately before the *caesura*, e.g. on the sixth syllable of an *alexandrine*. See also *elision* and the comments under *césure enjambante* about verse theorists.

Consonne d'appui: the consonant immediately preceding the *tonic vowel* in a *rime riche*.

Contre-assonance: the occurrence of words with different *tonic vowels* that are linked acoustically by identical consonants, e.g. "jase"/"brise."

Contre-rejet: the short word or phrase that falls into the *hemistich* or line before an *enjambment*, when the bulk of the relevant text comes after the enjambment.

Coupe: a device used in *scansion* to divide one *measure* from another within a line. The coupe usually falls immediately after the stressed syllable in a word. See also *coupe enjambante* and *coupe lyrique*.

Coupe enjambante: a *coupe* that divides a stressed word ending in a *mute e* into two, with the mute e counting as part of the following *measure*. For example, the six syllables in "un asi/le d'un jour" would be scanned as 3 + 3.

Coupe lyrique: a *coupe* that, in exceptional cases, falls after a stressed word ending in a *mute e*, normally because the word is isolated in terms of meaning and syntax. The mute e is included in the syllable count. For example, "Diane, / Séléné" would be scanned 3' + 3. An apostrophe denotes the presence of a coupe lyrique in scansion.

Decasyllable: a 10-syllable line, traditionally divided by a *caesura* into one section of 4 syllables and another of 6 syllables, although other combinations are possible (see Chapter 3).

Diaeresis: treating two contiguous vowels as 2 syllables for the purposes of syllable counting.

Distique: a *stanza* of 2 lines.

Dizain: a *stanza* of 10 lines. A dizain with a rhyme scheme *ababccdeed* is sometimes referred to as the major ode stanza.

E atone: see *mute e*.

E muet: see *mute e*.

Elision: when a *mute e* falls within a line but is followed by a word beginning with a vowel or unaspirated "h," it is "elided" or suppressed and does not count as a syllable.

Enjambment: when the sense and syntax of a verse text runs across the end of one *hemistich* or line into the next. See also *rejet* and *contre-rejet*.

Envoi: the short section at the end of a *ballade* where the poet addresses a rich or powerful figure such as a prince.

Feminine rhyme: a rhyme based on words in which the syllable bearing the main stress is followed by a *mute e*, e.g. mystère/sphère.

Hemistich: the two parts of a line in which a *caesura* is applied. In an *alexandrine*, both parts will be 6 syllables long.

Hiatus: the clash created where two vowels are found side-by-side, either within a word ("persu-ader") or in two successive words ("tu as"). Hiatus between words was considered bad poetic practice for much of the nineteenth century.

Huitain: a stanza of 8 lines.

Impair: a line with an odd number of syllables, e.g. 5, 7, 9 and so on.

Major ode stanza: see *dizain*.

Masculine rhyme: a rhyme based on words where the main stress falls on the final syllable and there is no following *mute e*, e.g. horizon/gazon.

Measure: a subdivision of a *hemistich* or line. The last syllable in a measure will normally carry a stress.

Minor ode stanza: see *sizain*.

Mute e: the syllables "e," "es," or "ent" at the end of words. These may or may not be included in the syllable count for the line depending on where they fall or what they are followed by. Also known as the e atone or e muet. See Chapter 2.

Octosyllable: an 8-syllable line.

Pair: a line with an even number of syllables, e.g. 4, 6, 8 and so on.

Pentameter: in English verse, a line with five feet.

Quatrain: a *stanza* of 4 lines, typically made up of *rimes croisées* or *rimes embrassées*.

Quintil: a *stanza* of 5 lines.

Rejet: the short word or phrase that falls into the following *hemistich* or line after an *enjambment*, when the bulk of the relevant text comes before the *enjambment*.

Rimes croisées: a pattern of alternating rhymes, found in *quatrains*, and notated as *abab*.

Rimes embrassées: a rhyme pattern found in *quatrains*, notated as *abba*.

Rime faible: see *rime pauvre*.

Rime léonine: a rhyme where the *tonic vowel*, any following consonant(s), any immediately preceding consonant(s), and at least one preceding vowel rhyme, e.g. breuvage/veuvage.

Rime pauvre: a rhyme where only the *tonic vowel* rhymes, e.g. vie/folie. Also known as rime faible.

Rime riche: a rhyme where the *tonic vowel*, any following consonant(s), and any immediately preceding consonant(s) rhyme, e.g. passe/espace.

Rime suffisante: a rhyme where the *tonic vowel* and any following consonant(s) rhyme, e.g. belle/immortelle.

Rimes plates: rhyming couplets, typically notated as *aabbccdd* and so on.

Rondel: one of the standard fixed poetic forms in French. See Chapter 5.

Scansion: the analysis of the meter of a verse text.

Sizain: a *stanza* of 6 lines. Where the sizain has a rhyme scheme *aabccb*, it is sometimes referred to as the minor ode stanza.

Sonnet: one of the standard fixed poetic forms in French. See Chapter 5.

Stanza: a grouping of lines within a poem, typically (though not always — see *terza rima*) containing a completed sequence of rhymes and separated from other stanzas by a blank space. Referred to as a strophe in French.

Strophe: see *stanza*.

Synaeresis: treating two contiguous vowels as one syllable for the purposes of syllable counting.

Tercet: a *stanza* of 3 lines.

Tercet monorime: a 3-line *stanza* where all the rhymes are the same.

Terza rima: a rhyme pattern of Italian origin where the middle rhyme of one three-line *stanza* becomes the first and third rhymes of the next. It is notated *aba bcb cdc* and so on. The pattern is usually closed by a single line that rhymes with the middle line of the previous stanza.

Tetrameter: in English, a line with 4 feet.

Tonic vowel: the vowel in a word or phrase on which the main stress falls.

Vers composé: a line of 9 syllables or more that is divided into two parts by a *caesura*.

Vers impair: see *impair*.

Vers libéré: verse written by poets such as Verlaine and Rimbaud, who broke away from traditional practice and introduced new freedoms into French verse forms. See Chapter 7.

Vers libre: the free verse that was published in France from 1886 onwards. See Chapter 7.

Vers libres classiques: a form of verse, mixing lines in different meters, used by poets such as La Fontaine. Also known as vers mêlés.

Vers mêlés: see *vers libres classiques*.

Vers pair: see *pair*.

Vers simple: a line of 8 syllables or less. The vers simple does not have a *caesura*.

Villanelle: one of the standard fixed forms in French. See Chapter 5.

Volta: the point in a *sonnet* where the subject matter takes a "turn"—for instance, where the poet steps back to explain the significance of the earlier parts of the poem. This is usually linked to the transition from the *quatrains* to the *tercets* within the sonnet. See Chapter 5.

Notes

Chapter 1

1. *The Singer as Interpreter: Claire Croiza's Master Classes*, edited and translated by B. Bannerman (London: Victor Gollancz, 1989), p. 19. Croiza is also credited with saying "To interpret, an intimate assimilation of the text is necessary."

2. Pierre Bernac, *The Interpretation of French Song* (London: Victor Gollancz, 1987), p. 3.

3. For an example, see Jean-Michel Nectoux's biography *Gabriel Fauré: A Musical Life* (Cambridge: Cambridge University Press, 1991), p. 392.

Chapter 2

1. Twelve-syllable lines had appeared in French as early as the twelfth century and in 1179 were used in *Li Romans d'Alixandre*, one of whose authors happened to be called Alexandre de Bernay. The line became formally known as the "alexandrin" in the fifteenth century.

2. As well as being mobile, these secondary stresses are optional and occasionally a hemistich may only contain one stress—the fixed one on its final syllable. For instance, in Fauré's song "Mai," to a text by Victor Hugo, we find the hemistich "Et le rayonnement," which we could interpret as having only one main stress, on "rayonnement." As we shall see later in the chapter, certain types of syllable, such as the mute e, cannot bear a stress.

3. The possible combinations of the alexandrine are $1 + 5 + 1 + 5, 1 + 5 + 2 + 4, 1 + 5 + 3 + 3$ and so on. If the possibility of a single-stress hemistich is taken into account (see note 2 above), the total number of possible combinations rises to thirty-six $(6 + 6, 6 + 1 + 5$ and so on).

4. Note that French verse theory does allow for other forms of accentuation, including accents that fall on the opening syllables of words or word groups (commonly referred to as "accents d'insistance" or "accents oratoires"). However, such accents are generally considered to be a personal choice of the reader, rather than something inherent in the verse.

5. From Shakespeare's "Sonnet XXXXIII," set by Britten. Note that this line has a feminine ending that does not form part of the meter.

6. From William Barnes's "My Orcha'd in Linden Lea," set by Vaughan Williams.

7. Some critics have argued strongly that French does have the equivalent of feet. For a highly technical discussion, see Roger Pensom, *Accent and Metre in French* (Bern: Peter Lang, 1998).

8. The concept of meter and its relationship to rhythm is a major topic in its own right. For further reading on verse in English, see Philip Hobsbaum, *Metre, Rhythm and Verse Form* (London: Routledge, 1996). For a discussion of meter and rhythm in French verse, see Clive Scott, *Reading the Rhythm* (Oxford: Oxford University Press, 1993), pp. 3-24.

9. Britten sets "battening" on three separate notes. Note that this line starts with a dactylic foot (long, short, short), an example of the poet creating rhythmic variation in a primarily iambic meter.

10. The mute e accounts for around a quarter of all potential French syllables according to scholars such as Mazaleyrat. See Jean Mazaleyrat, *Éléments de métrique française* (Paris: Armand Colin, 1990), p. 57.

11. A mute e at the end of a line also indicates a "feminine" rhyme. See Chapter 6.

12. The letter "h" at the beginning of a French word is categorized as being either "aspirated" or "unaspirated." An aspirated "h" acts as a consonant and prevents elision. For instance, in the second line of Fauré's "Les berceaux," "Que la houl(e) inclin(e) en silenc(e)," the "la" and "hou" in the phrase "la houle" count as two separate syllables, maintaining the 8-syllable meter.

13. The technical term for counting two contiguous vowels as one syllable is "synaeresis." The term for counting two contiguous vowels as two syllables is "diaeresis."

14. This is not the case in early French verse, written at a time when these syllables would have been pronounced in normal speech.

15. Note that the presence of a coupe lyrique is shown in scansion by an apostrophe.

16. Note that the "e" in words such as "vie" counts as a syllable unless it is elided. It was considered bad poetic practice during much of the nineteenth century to use the plurals of such words ("vies") where a vowel was immediately followed by a mute e that could not be elided.

17. In early French verse, we find examples of what is called the "césure épique." This caesura allows for the suppression of a mute e at the end of a measure in circumstances where the syllable would normally count. An example from the 10-syllable verse of the *Chanson de Roland* is "E li messag(e) // descendirent a pied." Note that the traditional 4 + 6 division of the decasyllable (discussed in Chapter 3) is preserved. Examples of the césure épique are rare in the nineteenth century mélodie because the practice was by then

frowned upon. However, the césure épique reappears in twentieth century verse.

18. Where the bulk of the relevant phrase comes *after* the enjambment, leaving a short word or phrase isolated on the previous line, the term used is "contre-rejet." The last stanza of Verlaine's "En sourdine" offers an example: ". . . le soir / Des chênes noirs tombera."

19. Note that phrases such as "Je l'ai vu(e) aussi" would be acceptable because of the intervening elision of the mute e.

Chapter 3

1. See Michel Décaudin, *Apollinaire* (Paris: Le Livre de Poche, 2002), p. 98.

2. See, for instance, Alain Frontier, *La poésie* (Paris: Belin, 1992), p. 161.

3. See Roy Lewis, *On Reading French Verse: A Study of Poetic Form* (Oxford: Oxford University Press, 1982), p. 47.

4. On the other hand, the second half of the line could be scanned as having only one main stress (on rencontrée), the 3 + 3 + 6 reading emphasizing the contrast between the poet's depressed state and the sudden rush of excitement at the new encounter. In this case, we might argue that the poet has created a rhythm in the line that counteracts the natural curve of the alexandrine.

5. On the other hand, there are many texts that use only the 4 + 6 meter. As a general rule, the different forms of the decasyllable tend not to be mixed in an individual poem, at least until the mid-nineteenth century; even later in the century one form usually predominates.

6. See, for instance, Clive Scott, *A Question of Syllables* (Cambridge: Cambridge University Press, 1986), p. 51.

7. For instance, Verlaine's "Mandoline," from the *Fêtes galantes*, is written in a 7-syllable meter. His "Chevaux de bois," from the collection *Romances sans paroles*, is an example of 9-syllable verse, evoking perhaps the music of the fairground. Both poems have been set by a number of composers.

8. This poem is found in Verlaine's collection *Jadis et naguère*. The translation is by Joanna Richardson.

Chapter 4

1. Throughout Chapters 4 and 5, I use the standard notation for designating stanzas based on rhyme schemes, in which a small *a* represents the first rhyme in a poem and a small *b* the second. A pattern *abab* means that we are looking at a 4-line stanza where the final words in verses 1 and 3 rhyme, as do the final words in lines 2 and 4.

2. Note that the syllable count varies in different parts of this poem. See Chapter 7 for a discussion of the way in which verse practice evolved during the late nineteenth and early twentieth centuries.

3. See Clive Scott, *French Verse-Art: A Study* (Cambridge: Cambridge University Press, 1980), p. 133.

4. Note the use of the alternative "poetic" spelling of "avecque," which allows the poet to maintain the 8-syllable line, but also adds phonetic weight to the word, helping to emphasize the interplay of light and shade.

5. The rhyme pattern is notated as *abab cdcd aeea* because the crucial rhyme words at the end of the first and third lines of the first stanza are repeated in the first and fourth lines of the third stanza.

Chapter 5

1. Although there are many variants, the traditional English or Shakespearean sonnet has a rhyme scheme *ababcdcdefefgg*—three quatrains, each with new rhymes, completed by a rhyming couplet. Some French poets, including Mallarmé (who was, of course, a teacher of English), experimented with this form of the sonnet.

2. Another example is Gautier's poem "La caravane," set by Chausson.

3. Another example is Debussy's setting of Verlaine's sonnet "Le son du cor s'afflige."

4. The volta is memorably underlined in Duparc's setting by the repetition of "C'est là."

5. See Henri Morier, *Dictionnaire de poétique et de rhétorique* (Paris: Presses Universitaires de France, 1998), p.1050.

6. Note that Berlioz's song "Villanelle," based on a Gautier text, is not really a villanelle in the traditional sense of the form, despite its title.

7. See, for instance, Clive Scott, *French Verse-Art: A Study* (Cambridge: Cambridge University Press, 1980), p. 159.

8. During the nineteenth century, poets such as Hugo created new forms of ballade. Here, I have concentrated on the traditional variants.

9. See, for instance, Henri Morier, *Dictionnaire de poétique et de rhétorique* (Paris: Presses Universitaires de France, 1998), p. 143.

Chapter 6

1. Throughout this chapter I focus primarily on the rhymes at the end of lines.

2. Théodore de Banville, *Petit traité de poésie française* (1872; reprint, Paris: Ressouvenances, 1998), p. 47.

3. Louis Quicherat, *Petit traité de versification française* (Paris: Hachette, 1895), p. 33.

4. There are a few exceptions to this rule. For instance, "aimer" (to love) is allowed to rhyme with "mer" (the sea) in what is known as a "rime normande." Exceptions such as these are often based on syllables that had the same pronunciation in earlier periods of French.

5. The chapter entitled "On Singing French" in Pierre Bernac's book *The Interpretation of French Song* (London: Victor Gollancz, 1987) is also essential reading.

6. English too offers some classification of rhyme—cosily/rosily can be described as a triple rhyme, for instance, because of the concordance of three syllables. However, such classifications are not part of a larger system. Also, more elaborate rhymes tend to seem contrived in English in a way that they do not in French.

7. Under the modern system, the more identical phonetic elements there are, whether they follow or precede the vowel, the richer the rhyme. So the rhyme "ombre"/"sombre" merely suffisante under the earlier classification, would be classified as riche because there are three identical phonetic elements—om, b, re.

8. Some poetic movements, such as the Parnassians, made a focus on rhyme—and the use of rime riche in particular—something of a manifesto commitment. Banville, in his *Petit traité de poésie française*, writes, "Vous ne devez n'employer jamais que des rimes absolument brillantes, exactes, solides et riches, dans lesquelles on trouve TOUJOURS la consonne d'appui" (Banville's emphasis). See page 74 of the Ressouvenances 1998 edition.

9. The repetition of rhyme words in these texts intensifies this effect, as does the presence of an unrhymed line in each stanza of "Il pleure dans mon cœur."

10. Words ending in "aient" or "oient" are a special case. In the present tense (for instance, "voient" from the verb "voir") they count as feminine and their final 'ent' is classed as a separate syllable. In the imperfect or conditional tenses or the subjunctive mood, the final "aient" or "oient" is regarded as one syllable and the rhyme is masculine. Words ending in "ée" form feminine rhymes.

11. In old French pronunciation, the final "e" on feminine rhymes would have been sounded, differentiating masculine and feminine rhymes more fully, rather like English.

12. Clearly, if the poem had started with a masculine rhyme, the sequence of rhymes would have been reversed.

13. Note how the sequence of masculine and feminine rhymes in this poem (in rimes embrassées) differs from the Samain poem above—another source of contrast between the two main types of quatrain.

14. Note also the concentration of m and r sounds in this first line.

15. One important rule is sometimes referred to as "the law of potential liaison." Combinations such as "effort"/"sors" and "blanc"/"tremblant" were forbidden on the basis that the sounds produced by their final consonants (even if they were not sounded) would be different when in liaison with a following word beginning with a vowel or unaspirated h. Plurals such as "blancs"/"tremblants" were acceptable as rhymes, however, because they would both produce an "s" in liaison.

16. Roy Lewis calls these "amplified rhymes" in his book *On Reading French Verse* (Oxford: Oxford University Press, 1982).

17. The contrast between the 12- and 7-syllable meters has a similar effect, of course. See Chapter 4.

Chapter 7

1. The Romantics were not the first to use this form of the alexandrine; examples of a tripartite structure can be found in earlier poets (including La Fontaine). However, poets such as Hugo used this device in a more consistent and programmatic way.

2. Or even a 4 + 8 reading, which would emphasize the swirling combination of earth, air, and sea.

3. See Chapter 1 for a discussion of this device.

4. Note also that in poems such as Verlaine's "Donc, ce sera . . .," set by Fauré, which contain sequences of decasyllables, the caesura is increasingly mobile and no longer divides the lines into the traditional patterns of 4 + 6 or 5 + 5 (see Chapter 3).

5. For a comprehensive history of the vers libre, see Clive Scott, *Vers Libre: The Emergence of Free Verse in France 1886–1914* (Oxford: Oxford University Press, 1990).

6. See Clive Scott, "French Versification: A Summary," in *Nineteenth Century French Poetry*, ed. Christopher Prendergast (Cambridge: Cambridge University Press, 1990), p. 255.

7. "Bleuet" was set by Poulenc. The layout of the poem can be seen on p. 375 of Graham Johnson and Richard Stokes, *A French Song Companion* (Oxford: Oxford University Press, 2000). In earlier French poetry, changes in margins had traditionally highlighted a change in meter. This is clearly not the case in Apollinaire's poem. Note also that Apollinaire suppresses all punctuation in this and many of his other poems.

8. See Chapter 2 for a discussion of the traditional ways of handling the mute e and of the concepts of "synaeresis" and "diaeresis." Modern poets reintroduced into their verse many of the practices of early French verse that had been proscribed between the sixteenth and late nineteenth centuries. These included the "césure enjambante" (where an unelided mute e is placed immediately after the caesura, e.g. on the seventh syllable of an alexandrine), the "césure lyrique" (where an unelided mute e is placed immediately before the caesura, e.g. on the sixth syllable of an alexandrine) and the "césure épique" (where a mute e that cannot be elided—and would therefore have counted as a syllable—is nonetheless suppressed immediately before the caesura). In the Éluard poem that follows, we could argue that we are considering applying a form of césure épique.

9. The technical term for suppressing a mute e at the end of a word is "apocope," while the term "syncope" is used where a mute e is suppressed within a word.

10. A similar procedure would also need to be applied to the last line of the poem. This still leaves the 4-syllable twelfth line as something of an anomaly in the poem.

11. Fauré's settings of Van Lerberghe also contain many regular lines and rhymes.

12. Many commentators refer to the relationship between the mute e and traditional French poetic diction and suggest that when poets neglect or suppress the mute e, they may be deliberately bringing the language of their verse closer to prose or to everyday speech. See, for example, Alain Frontier, *La poésie* (Paris: Belin, 1992), p. 117.

13. Debates continue among scholars about whether a regular 12-syllable line in a free verse poem can really be read as an alexandrine or merely as a free verse line that happens to contain 12 syllables.

14. Set by Britten. There remain questions over whether this should be classified as a poem or a prose-poem. See Clive Scott, *Vers Libre: The Emergence of Free Verse in France 1886–1914* (Oxford: Oxford University Press, 1990), pp. 181-99 for a detailed discussion.

15. Poets such as Kahn talked in terms of recurring syllabic groups of equal length ("constantes syllabiques") as the basis of modern verse. However, Kahn did not necessarily envisage lines of Desnos's dimensions.

Appendix 1

1. Hugo's original line runs "Tu marches donc sans cesse! Oh! que n'es-tu de ceux," a regular alexandrine.

2. Graham Johnson and Richard Stokes, *A French Song Companion* (Oxford University Press, 2000), p. 31.

3. F. W. J. Hemmings, *Culture and Society in France 1789–1848* (Leicester, 1987), p. 219.

4. An alternative reading would be that the fragmented syntax in lines 10 and 11 reflects the frustrated ambitions of the dreamers that are (at least to some extent) assuaged in the balanced 4 + 4 structure of line 12.

5. Fauré changes "fondons" to "mêlons."

Suggestions for Further Reading

Two essential general books on French song are Pierre Bernac's *The Interpretation of French Song*, re-issued most recently in paperback by Kahn & Averill in 1997, and Graham Johnson and Richard Stokes's inexhaustible *A French Song Companion*, published in 2000 by Oxford University Press.

The leading scholar of French versification writing in English is undoubtedly Clive Scott. His *French Verse-Art: A Study* (Cambridge: Cambridge University Press, 1980) remains perhaps his most accessible book on the subject. Later publications, such as *Vers Libre: The Emergence of Free Verse in France 1886–1914* (Oxford: Oxford University Press, 1990), address more specific topics. Roy Lewis, meanwhile, has produced a valuable one-volume introduction to French verse specifically addressed at students, called *On Reading French Verse: A Study of Poetic Form* (Oxford: Oxford University Press, 1982). A more recent guide is Mary Lewis Shaw's *The Cambridge Introduction to French Poetry* (Cambridge: Cambridge University Press, 2003).

For anyone wishing to explore French views of their versification, Théodore de Banville's *Petit traité de poésie française*, originally published in 1872 and re-issued in 1998 by Ressouvenances, remains a core text. More recent general introductions include Michèle Aquien's *La versification* (Paris: Presses Universitaires de France, 1990; 4th edition 1998), Jean Mazaleyrat's *Éléments de métrique française* (Paris: Armand Colin, 1965; 7th edition 1990), and Jean-Michel Gouvard's *La versification* (Paris: Presses Universitaires de France, 1999). Henri Morier's *Dictionnaire de poétique et de rhétorique* (Paris: Presses Universitaires de France, 1961; 5th edition 1998) is still unrivaled in its detailed analysis of technical terms.

Finally, James Fenton's *An Introduction to English Poetry* (London: Penguin / Viking, 2002) is a good starting point for comparing and contrasting approaches to versification in French and English.

Index

Alexandrine: alexandrin tétramètre, 7; alexandrin trimètre, 70–71; different combinations of segments, 7, 108 ch.2 n.3; history, 10, 17, 70–71, 72, 108 ch.2 n.1, 113 n.1; structure and impact on reader, 17–18; rules governing, 6–7, 108 ch.2 n.2

Apollinaire, Guillaume: *Alcools*, 17; and the octosyllable, 21; and the quintil, 35–36; and traditional verse, 76; poems: 1904, 36; Bleuet, 74, 113 n.7; Dans le jardin d'Anna, 73; L'écrevisse, 61; Sanglots, 77–78

Aragon, Louis: *Du sonnet*, 44; and the French tradition, 76–77; C, 77

Arvers, Félix: Sonnet, 43

Aspirated h: 21, 109 n.12

Baïf, Jean-Antoine de: O ma belle rebelle, 27

Ballade: ballade primitive, 51–52; envoi, 52, 53, 54; grande ballade, 53–54; history and structure, 51–54; petite ballade, 52–53; technical challenges, 54

Banville, Théodore de: and the ron-

del, 45; and rhyme, 55, 56, 112 n.8; *Petit traité de poésie française*, 55; poems: La dernière pensée de Weber, 23; L'enamourée, 32; Le printemps, 47; Les étoiles, 48; Le thé, 47; Pierrot, 58–59

Baudelaire, Charles: and the couplet, 27–28; poems: La vie antérieure, 43–44, 67, 111 ch.5 n.4; Le jet d'eau, 40; Les hiboux, 57; L'invitation au voyage, 24, 39–40; Recueillement, 7

Bédat de Monlaur, Pierre: Le château du Bartas, 49–50

Béranger, Pierre Jean de: 24

Berlioz, Hector: La captive, 37; Sur les lagunes (Ma belle amie est morte), 10–11

Bernac, Pierre: 3, 112 n.5

Bizet, Georges: Adieux de l'hôtesse arabe, 23; Ma vie a son secret (Sonnet), 43

Bonnières, Robert de: Le manoir de Rosemonde, 43

Britten, Benjamin: Marine, 78, 114 n.14; The Kraken, 9

Caesura: in alexandrine, 6, 17–18, 70–71, 72; in decasyllable, 19–20, 113 n.4; types, 109–110 n.17, 113 n.8

Index

Caplet, André: Le corbeau et le renard, 69–70

Chabrier, Emmanuel: Ballade des gros dindons, 52; Le pas d'armes du roi Jean, 22, 37; L'invitation au voyage, 24, 39–40; Villanelle des petits canards, 50–51

Charles d'Orléans: Pour ce que Plaisance est morte, 46–47, 48; Quand je fus pris au pavillon, 45–46

Chausson, Ernest: Chanson perpétuelle, 35; La caravane, 44–45, 111 ch.5 n.2; Le colibri, 19–20, 43; Nanny, 23; *Serres chaudes*, 76

Coupe enjambante: 12, 13

Coupe lyrique: 13

Couplet: features, 28–29; history, 26–27; types, 27–28

Croiza, Claire: 3, 108 ch.1 n.1

Cros, Charles: Nocturne, 35

Debussy, Claude: Ballade des femmes de Paris, 52–53; Ballade que Villon feit à la requeste de sa mère pour prier Nostre-Dame, 53–54; Chevaux de bois, 110 n.7; Clair de lune, 14–15; Colloque sentimentale, 28–29; En sourdine, 3–4, 64–65, 110 n.18; Green, 16, 66; Il pleure dans mon cœur, 22, 59, 112 n.9; Le jet d'eau, 40; Le promenoir des deux amants, 29–30; Le son du cor s'afflige, 111 ch.5 n.3; L'ombre des arbres dans la rivière embrumée, 40, 66, 67; Mandoline, 66, 68, 71–72, 110 n.7; Nuit d'étoiles (La dernière pensée de Weber), 23; Pierrot, 58–59; Pour ce que Plaisance est morte, 46–47, 48; Recueillement, 7; Soupir, 72; Spleen, 39

Decasyllable: forms, 19–20, 110 n.5; history, 10, 18–19; links to song, 20; rhythmic uncertainty, 20

Desnos, Robert: Les espaces du sommeil, 79

Dizain: forms and internal organisation, 33–34; as major ode stanza, 33

Dominique, Jean: Le don silencieux, 26–27

Duparc, Henri: Au pays où se fait la guerre, 34; Chanson triste, 21; Lamento, 23; La vie antérieure, 43–44, 67, 111 ch.5 n.4; Le manoir de Rosemonde, 43; L'invitation au voyage, 24, 39–40; Phidylé, 59–60, 66; Soupir, 22

Elision: 11

Éluard, Paul: Jacques Villon, 74–75; Rayons des yeux et des soleils, 75–76

Enescu, George: Languir me fais (Chanson XIII), 19

English verse: counting syllables in, 9; differences to French verse, 7–10; feet, 8–9; iambic pentameter, 8; iambic tetrameter, 8; stress, meter and rhythm in, 7–9, 12

Enjambment: across stanzas, 71–72; effects of, 15; different impact in English and French verse, 14; within lines, 15

Index

Fauré, Gabriel: À Clymène, 23; Arpège, 62–63; Au bord de l'eau, 23; Au cimetière, 23; Chanson, 56; Clair de lune, 14–15; Dans la forêt de septembre, 64; Dans les ruines d'une abbaye, 58; Diane, Séléné, 13; Donc, ce sera . . . , 113 n.4; En sourdine, 3–4, 64–65, 110 n.18; Green, 16, 66; J'allais par des chemins perfides, 34–35; La chanson du pêcheur (Lamento), 10–11; La lune blanche, 22, 38; La mer est infinie, 18; La rose, 20; Le don silencieux, 26–27; Le papillon et la fleur, 22–23; Le parfum impérissable, 43; Les berceaux (Le long du quai), 4, 30–31, 109 n.12; Les roses d'Ispahan, 7; Mai, 108 ch.2 n.2; Mandoline, 66, 68, 71–72, 110 n.7; N'est-ce pas?, 35; Prison (Le ciel est, par-dessus le toit), 59; Quand tu plonges tes yeux dans mes yeux, 28; Rencontre, 18; Vaisseaux . . . , 15

Free verse: challenges syllable counting, 75–76; early innovations, 69–72; expresses the poet's mind, 73; impact, 76–77; and layout of poems, 73–74, 113 n.7; and line lengths, 73; origins, 73; and rhyming, 74–75; ways of reading, 77–79

French verse: common metres, 17–25; counting syllables in, 9–12, 109 n.16; differences to English verse, 7–10; the French line, 6–16; mixed metres in, 23; poetic language in, 15–16, 111 ch.4 n.4; stress, meter and rhythm in, 7–9, 12, 108 ch.2 n.4

Gautier, Théophile: and the decasyllable, 19; poems: Infidelité, 32; La caravane, 44–45, 111 ch.5 n.2; Lamento (Connaissez-vous la blanche tombe), 23; Lamento (Ma belle amie est morte), 10–11; Romance (Au pays où se fait la guerre), 34

Gérard, Rosemonde: Villanelle des petits canards, 50–51

Gounod, Charles: L'absent, 23; Le premier jour de mai, 33; Le soir, 60; Le vallon, 12, 14; O ma belle rebelle, 27; Venise, 62

Grandmougin, Charles: Rencontre, 18

Hahn, Reynaldo: Chanson d'automne, 32–33; D'une prison (Le ciel est, par-dessus le toit), 59; En sourdine, 3–4, 12, 64–65, 110 n.18; Fêtes galantes (Mandoline), 66, 68, 71–72, 110 n.7; Infidelité, 32; La bonne chanson (La dure épreuve va finir), 28; L'enamourée, 32; Le printemps, 47; Les étoiles, 48; L'heure exquise (La lune blanche), 22, 38; Paysage triste (L'ombre des arbres dans la rivière embrumée), 40, 66, 67; Mes vers fuiraient doux et frêles, 24; Offrande (Green), 16, 66; Quand je fus pris au pavillon, 45–46;

Index

Hahn, Reynaldo (*continued*)
Quand la nuit n'est pas
étoilée, 29
Hexasyllable: 11, 21, 22
Hiatus: 15
Honegger, Arthur: Le château du
Bartas, 49–50; *Saluste du
Bartas*, 49
Hugo, Victor: and the alexandrine,
70–71; poems: Adieux de l'
hôtesse arabe, 23; À une
femme, 70–71; Attente, 36;
Dans les ruines d'une abbaye,
58; La captive, 37; Le papil-
lon et la fleur, 22–23; Le
pas d'armes du roi Jean, 22,
37; Mai, 108 ch.2 n.2; Mes
vers fuiraient doux et frêles
24; Oh! quand je dors, 19;
Quand la nuit n'est pas
étoilée, 29
Huitain: 37

Invocations: 13

Koechlin, Charles: Le thé, 47

La Fontaine, Jean de: Le corbeau et
le renard, 69–70
Lahor, Jean: Chanson triste, 21.
Lamartine, Alphonse de: Le soir, 60;
Le vallon, 12, 14
La Ville de Mirmont, Jean de: Diane,
Séléné, 13; La mer est infinie,
18; Vaisseaux . . . , 15
Leconte de Lisle, Charles-Marie-
René: and the decasyllable,
19; and the villanelle, 49;
poems: La rose, 20; Le colibri,
19–20, 43; Le parfum im-
périssable, 43; Les roses d'Is-
pahan, 7; Nanny, 23; Phidylé,
59–60, 66

Leguerney, Jacques: À sa maîtresse (À
Cassandre), 24
Liszt, Franz: Enfant, si j'étais roi (À
une femme) 70–71; Oh!
quand je dors, 19
Lutoslawski, Witold: Les espaces du
sommeil, 79

Mallarmé, Stéphane: and the vers
libéré, 71–72; poems: Soupir,
72; Surgi de la croupe et du
bond, 41–42
Marot, Clément: Chanson XIII, 19.
Mendès, Catulle: Dans la forêt de
septembre, 64
Morand, Paul: Chanson romanesque,
63–64
Musset, Alfred de: Venise, 62.
Mute e: frequency in French, 109
n.10; and poetic diction, 114
n.12; rules governing the,
10–12; scanning the, 12–13;
treatment after a caesura,
13–14

Octosyllable: history, 20–21; links to
speech and song, 21; rhyth-
mic ambiguity in, 21; struc-
ture, 21

Passerat, Jean: Ode du premier jour
de mai, 33
Poulenc, Francis: 1904, 36; Bleuet,
74, 113 n.7; C, 77; Dans le
jardin d'Anna, 73; Jacques
Villon, 74–75; L'écrevisse, 61;
Rayons des yeux et des soleils,
75–76; Sanglots, 77–78

Quatrain: rimes croisées form of, 29;
rimes embrassées form of,
29–30; switching between
forms of, 30–31

Index

Quicherat, Louis: 55
Quintil: history and features, 35–36;
    use by Apollinaire, 35–36

Ravel, Maurice: Chanson ro-
    manesque, 63–64; Soupir, 72;
    Surgi de la croupe et du
    bond, 41–42
Régnier, Henri de: Chanson, 56
Richepin, Jean: Au cimetière, 23
Rhyme: alternation of rhyme gen-
    ders, 62–65, 113 nn.12–13;
    and assonance, 57; as the
    essential feature of French
    verse, 55–56; masculine and
    feminine rhymes, 60, 112
    nn.10–11; qualities of differ-
    ent rhyme genders, 61; rhyme
    degree, 57–60, 112 nn.6–8;
    rules of rhyming, 56–57, 65,
    111 ch.6 n.4, 112 n.15; and
    the Symbolists, 56
Rimbaud, Arthur: and the vers libéré,
    71–72; Marine, 78, 114 n.14
Rondel: disappearance of refrain, 48;
    history and structure, 45–46,
    47–48; technical challenges,
    46; unity of form, 46–47
Ronsard, Pierre de: À Cassandre, 24
Rostand, Edmond: Ballade des gros
    dindons, 52

Saint-Saëns, Camille: L'attente, 36;
    Le pas d'armes du roi Jean,
    22, 37
Samain, Albert: Arpège, 62–63
Septain: 36–37
Séverac, Déodat de: Les hiboux,
    57
Short lines: combinations of, 23; as
    complementary meters,
    22–23; as meters in their
    own right, 22

Sizain: forms and internal organisa-
    tion, 32–33; as minor ode
    stanza, 32
Sonnet: history and structure, 41–43,
    111 ch.5 n.1; patterns within,
    44–45; variations, 44–45;
    volta, 44–45
Sound patterning: devices, 66–67;
    effects, 67–68
Stanzas: and punctuation and typog-
    raphy, 34, 38–39; reasons for,
    26; and syntax, 32–33, 38;
    types of, 26–37; and variations
    in meter, 39–40
Sully Prudhomme: Au bord de l'eau,
    23; Le long du quai (Les
    berceaux), 4, 30–31, 109 n.12;
    Soupir, 22

Tennyson, Alfred: The Kraken, 9
Tercet: and Symbolists, 35; tercet
    monorime form, 35; terza
    rima form, 34–35
Thomas, Dylan: 48
Tristan l'Hermite: Le promenoir des
    deux amants, 29–30

Van Lerberghe, Charles: Quand tu
    plonges tes yeux dans mes
    yeux, 28
Verlaine, Paul: and the alexandrine,
    6; and the couplet, 27–28;
    and the decasyllable, 19; and
    rhyme, 65; and the vers
    libéré, 71–72; poems: À
    Clymène, 23; Art poétique,
    24; Chanson d'automne,
    32–33, 38; Chevaux de bois,
    110 n.7; Clair de lune, 14–15;
    Colloque sentimentale,
    28–29; Donc, ce sera . . . ,
    113 n.4; En sourdine, 3–4, 12,
    64–65, 110 n.18; Green, 16,

Index

Verlaine, Paul (*continued*)
66; Il pleure dans mon cœur,
22, 59, 112 n.9; J'allais par des
chemins perfides, 34–35; La
dure épreuve va finir, 28; La
lune blanche, 38; Le ciel est,
par-dessus le toit, 59; Le son
du cor s'afflige, 111 ch.5 n.3;
L'ombre des arbres dans la
rivière embrumée, 40, 66, 67;
Mandoline, 66, 68, 71–72,
110 n.7; N'est-ce pas?, 35;
Spleen, 39
Vers composés: 17, 23
Vers impairs: association with music,
24; history of, 23–24; links to
new types of poetry, 24–25, 71
Vers libéré: 71–72
Vers libre: 69–79. *See* Free verse
Vers libres classiques (vers mêlés):
69–70
Vers simples: 17, 23
Villanelle: history and structure,
48–50; refrains, 51; technical
challenges, 51; variations,
49–50
Villon, François: and the petite bal-
lade, 52; Ballade des femmes
de Paris, 52–53; Ballade pour
prier Nostre Dame, 53–54